Make Money Online:

Roadmap of a dot com mogul

John Chow with Michael Kwan

New York

Make Money Online
A Roadmap to Becoming a Dot Com Mogul

Cover Design by: 3 Dog Design
              www.3dogdesign.net

ISBN 978-1-60037-673-3

Library of Congress Control Number: 2009931500

MORGAN · JAMES
THE ENTREPRENEURIAL PUBLISHER

Morgan James Publishing
1225 Franklin Ave., STE 325
Garden City, NY 11530-1693
Toll Free 800-485-4943
www.MorganJamesPublishing.com

In an effort to support local communities, raise awareness and funds, Morgan James Publishing donates one percent of all book sales for the life of each book to Habitat for Humanity. Get involved today, visit **www.HelpHabitatForHumanity.org**.

Table of Contents

Foreword by Joel Comm v

Preface. vii

Chapter One: The Best Time to Get Started. 1

Chapter Two: My Story 6

Chapter Three: Blogging 101 19

Chapter Four: Ten Essential Blogging Tips. 26

Chapter Five: WordPress Basics 35

Chapter Six: WordPress Techniques and Tools 43

Chapter Seven: Content is King. 56

Chapter Eight: Promotion and Search Engine Optimization 71

Chapter Nine: The Importance of Branding. 95

Chapter Ten: Optimizing Google AdSense. 106

Chapter Eleven: My Top Moneymakers 122

Chapter Twelve: Private Ad Sales 130

Chapter Thirteen: The Formula for Success 140

Appendix: Useful Links. 145

About the Authors. 147

Bonus 149

Foreword

When the mainstream media discuss doing business online, names such as Yahoo!, eBay, Amazon, and Google are frequently mentioned. We hear about the big companies that are doing big business, and may be led to believe that these behemoths are the core of online commerce. On the contrary, I believe that just as the middle class drives our economy, it is the small businessperson that is truly responsible for the incredible growth of the Internet.

Nowhere is this demonstrated more clearly than in the case of John Chow.

After developing a technology site that has become one of the most popular of its kind, John focused his attention on becoming a prolific blogger. While he may never have seen the fame and fortune that would soon follow, his passion for his subject matter has naturally connected with thousands of readers and has earned him a name in the industry.

It's this passion that you'll find oozing from every page of this book. John speaks about blogging from a point of authority. As one of the first bloggers to write about making money online by demonstrating exactly how he does it, and by publicly documenting his revenue streams each month on his blog, John has succeeded in connecting with the stay-at-home entrepreneur who wishes to achieve similar success.

Among the unique tools John uses to monetize his blog are Google AdSense, CPA ads, banner ads, and pay-per-review. Website owners should pay close attention to John's strategies, as I believe they are very duplicable.

It's true that the mainstream media has yet to catch on to the thousands of individuals who have kissed their jobs good-bye and replaced them with the freedom of enjoying profits from their own online businesses. As people like John Chow share their stories with the rest of the world, it's my hope that others will have the courage to seize the opportunity and begin writing their own success stories.

Who knows? The next time you see a news story about money being made on the Internet, don't be surprised to see John Chow's name in the headline.

Live Life Today!

Joel Comm

Preface

You may have noticed that this book has two authors. While I, John Chow, provided most of the ideas, techniques, and advice described in this book, it took Michael Kwan to put it all together in a comprehensive and comprehensible package. If you're a regular reader of John Chow Dot Com, you may have noticed a few posts written by Michael as well. Even so, the entirety of this book will be from my perspective. This only makes sense, since you want to hear the advice from a successful dot-com mogul. Enjoy!

Chapter One:
The Best Time to Get Started

In this chapter, you'll learn about finding the best time to get started with a new venture, what it means to wait for the perfect conditions, and the concept of someday.

According to Technorati, a trusted authority on what is happening on the World Wide Web right now, there are over one hundred million blogs on the Internet. It seems that nearly everyone has a blog these days, from celebrities like Martha Stewart and Ross the Intern to your ten-year-old neighbor down the street. The accessibility of the platform has made it increasingly easy for people to claim their own plots of online real estate, and they can use that space to talk about politics, sports, or what they had for lunch. The choice is 100 percent yours. If you've got something to say, blog about it, and your words can be read by literally millions and millions of people.

However, of these one hundred million blogs, very few make much money. In fact, the vast majority make no money whatsoever. But that's not what you want, is it? You want to make some real money blogging, and that's why you bought this book in the first place. Congratulations! You've already completed the first step on your path to becoming a dot-com mogul. Now you just have to read the book and implement the strategies described within.

If this was your average, run of the mill, get-rich-quick kind of book, this is probably where you'd be told how you'll be making mounds of money with less than an hour of work each day. They'd tell you how you can escape the nine-to-five lifestyle and be your own boss. They'd tell you about all the free time that you'll have and about all the unfathomable riches that you'd be enjoying during that free time. If you're looking to get rich quick, this might not be the book for you. The fact of the matter is that there is no such thing as a get-rich-quick scheme. I am not a get-rich-quick guru, nor do I do want to be associated with them. I don't make money selling people on stupid schemes that lead to nowhere; I make money on the Internet with real websites.

The single greatest piece of advice that I can give you is to take action now. Not tomorrow. Not next week. Right now. Let me tell you why.

Someday Never Comes

Do you know how to tell a successful person from an unsuccessful one? Just take a look at the language that they use. When you talk to a successful person about his goals, he'll tell you exactly what he plans to achieve, what he plans to do to achieve it, and when he will do it. When an unsuccessful person answers this kind of question, assuming that he has any real goals to begin with, you're more likely to hear a response along the lines of "I hope to do this someday." But in reality, someday never comes.

The reason why a person uses words and phrases like *someday, I hope,* or *I wish*? It's because this gives him an out. This excuse allows him to avoid being held accountable for his actions and, ultimately, his failures. If he were to place a time limit on the goal and doesn't manage to achieve this goal, guess what? He fails. Some people hate to face failure and will do everything they can to avoid it. For example, if you say that you will become a millionaire *someday*, you literally have until you're buried six feet under to achieve this goal. Even if you ultimately fail to become a millionaire in the end, you won't be around to feel the pain of failure. In contrast, winners have no fear of failing in the short-term because they know that success comes from a string of failures. The key is to learn from your mistakes, learn from your failures, and build success from them.

Everyone has dreams and goals. The only real difference between a dream and a goal is the fact that a goal is a dream with a timeline and a plan of action. We all have dreams—becoming financially independent, having a happy family, contributing to society in the best way possible—but how many of you have made it a goal to achieve these dreams? How many of you have placed a time limit on each of these dreams? Or did you just say that you're going to do it *someday*?

Think about this way. Can you imagine buying a presale condominium and not knowing when it will be completed? Imagine if you were to approach the developer about the matter and the only response that they'd give you is, "It'll be finished someday." Who would even consider buying into a condominium like that? You have to think about your dreams in the same way. By telling yourself that your dream will come true someday or that you *hope* that it will come true someday, you're effectively giving the same response as the condo developer. If you're not willing to buy the condo, why on earth would you be willing to buy your dream?

If you wish to achieve anything in life, you have to place a time limit on it. A goal without a time limit is not a goal. A time limit forces you to take action *right now*, instead of just sitting on the couch waiting for things to happen. Don't be afraid to fail because without the risk of failure, it is not possible to achieve any sort of real success. Failure is required in order to succeed. You will not find a successful person who doesn't have a few good stories to tell about their failures. Take a look at someone like Donald Trump. As much as some people would like to believe otherwise, Trump is not infallible. The real estate mogul has come close to bankruptcy on several occasions, and there are very few failures that are worse than bankruptcy. Despite these, "the Donald" is still respected as one of the savviest businesspeople on the planet. He learns from his failures and continues to succeed in a monumental way.

Ducks and the Waiting Game

Don't give yourself an out through a foolish excuse either. Are you the kind of person who likes to wait until everything is perfect before starting a new venture? There are tons of people out there who are just like this, holding off on buying that house or investing in that stock because they are hoping that the market conditions will soon be changing in their favor. They hold off on starting a new business because the economy isn't quite right. They hold off on getting married because they're still trying to save enough money for that big wedding. Insert whatever excuse you want; most of these people are still waiting. Don't wait. The perfect time is right now.

Success comes to those who make opportunities happen, not those who sit around waiting for opportunities to fall into their laps. If you're waiting for all your ducks to line up before going forward with making money online, that's all you'll be doing: waiting. The fact of the matter is that the ducks are never going to line up for you. The conditions will never be completely perfect. If I had waited until everything was just right before starting my first money-making website, the TechZone, I would still be waiting to this day.

When you really dig deep and look at the things that are keeping you from where you want to be, you'll find that it's not the economy, the market, other people, or anything to do with a few ducks. The only thing that's keeping you from being where you want to be is the person staring at you in the mirror. Some people are always looking for external conditions on which to blame their current situations because they don't want to accept responsibility for them. They don't want to say that they failed. Consider the word *responsibility*. Responsibility refers to the ability to choose your response. In any situation that you're faced with, you have the ability to choose how you respond. Responsible people don't need to have all their ducks in a row because they are able to work through a series of disorganized fowl.

Making Money Online

Making a living off the Internet is something that many people want to do. There are innumerable folks on the Web that desperately want to make enough money from their blogs to be able to quit their day jobs. It's something that many of my friends dream of doing. However, after all these years, only two have managed to actually do it. You know why? They actually listened to me when I told them to build a site. They built their sites to the best of their abilities and learned a lot along the way. Sure, they have suffered a failure here and there, but they are certainly much more successful *because* of it. When it comes to the other people to whom I gave the same basic advice—"Go build a site!"—they sure sounded positive. They would say things like, "Yeah! Sounds great, I need to do this. Working at a job sucks!"

I'm still waiting to see the sites. I'm sure they'll get to it *someday*.

Chapter Two:
My Story

In this chapter, you'll learn a little about how I became a dot-com mogul, how I got into the world of blogging, and how much money I made in the first month I monetized my blog.

I f you had told me five years ago that I would be making over $30,000 a month from my personal blog, I probably wouldn't have believed you. I have been making money online for a number of years now, but this was largely through a commercial site called The TechZone. I've learned much from the rise, fall, and reemergence of that site, and I've taken these lessons to John Chow Dot Com. Even so, I would have never imagined that my personal blog would become quite as popular as it has. Coupling my experience from the TechZone with my experience with John Chow Dot Com, I think it's fair to say that I know a thing or two about how to make money online. Even so, I had humble beginnings like anyone else. One of the greatest keys to success, you see, is starting with something that you are passionate about. If you are truly passionate about something and are willing to work hard to achieve your goals, success will surely follow.

But how did I get started and how did John Chow Dot Com evolve to what it is today? Let me share my story with you, along with some of the lessons that I learned along the way.

Moto's Project 504

It was in 1999 that I built my first computer all by myself. Naturally, I was rather proud of this achievement, so I decided to start a personal home page that described what I did and how I did it. I called it Moto's Project 504. Moto is the nickname that I used, and continue to use, in many of my online endeavors—posting in forums and so forth—and the Project 504 part? Well, that's because the first computer that I built by myself was a Pentium II 300, overclocked all the way to 504 MHz, which was a feat unheard of at the time. It was an exercise in what was possible, and I wanted to share this achievement with the rest of the Internet community. I also wanted to gloat a little. In any case, the site was created using Microsoft FrontPage because I didn't know any HTML whatsoever. It wasn't the prettiest thing in the world, but it worked. And oh boy, did it work.

The Project 504 home page got about two hundred page views on its first day, and most of the traffic came from a forum where I was a member. To this day, forums remain a significant source of traffic for many successful websites, and I highly encourage anyone looking to make money from a website to be actively involved in related forums. This is because of the community that can develop within a popular forum, which is a place where like-minded individuals from around the world can bounce ideas off of one another and otherwise communicate in a manner that just wouldn't be possible without the Internet. The forum that was sending traffic to Project 504, Riva 3D, was one of the biggest NVIDIA forums on the Web. It's no longer in business, but it was a monster in 1999. NVIDIA is one of the world's largest manufacturers of computer graphics cards, but I was the guy on the forum who kept proclaiming the superiority of 3DFX, one of NVIDIA's competitors. This made life a living hell for all the NVIDIA enthusiasts, because I would always attack their love of NVIDIA. In the end, I guess they got the last laugh when NVIDIA bought out 3DFX in 2000. I didn't care, of course, because Moto's Project 504 was garnering a fair bit of attention, and I loved having my fun with the NVIDIA fanboys.

As Project 504 became more popular, I tried to add more content to the site by posting news from other tech sites. There weren't nearly as many tech sites around in those days as there are today. The biggest and best-known tech news site of the day was probably Tom's Hardware, followed by AnandTech. After about a week of posting news from around the Web, the strangest thing happened: websites started e-mailing me their news. Naturally, I was very happy about this turn of events, because it meant that I didn't have to go looking for news anymore. The news came to me, and Project 504 continued to grow.

One day, I received a news release from Mike Chambers, an NVIDIA fanboy who I knew through the Riva 3D forum. Mike sent out this news release with all the e-mail addresses in the carbon copy (CC) field (as opposed to the blind carbon copy ([BCC]) field). What this means is that all the thirty or so e-mail addresses were fully visible! Here's a quick note to anyone who sends out news releases: use the blind carbon copy (BCC) field for all the recipients! These thirty e-mail addresses gave birth to my first news mailing list. Today that news list has over one thousand addresses (and growing).

The TechZone is Born

Even though the Internet wasn't nearly as developed back then as it is today, things still moved quickly. After about a month, I decided that Project 504 needed its own domain name. I created a post asking readers for recommendations, and I think I received about a dozen replies. In the end, none of the suggested names appealed to me. I racked my brain for ideas and then it dawned on me. At the time, I also owned a site called The LoveZone, which served as a home page for members of a certain chat room. Giving it a little bit of thought, it came to me that I could extend this idea. LoveZone? How about TechZone? Sometimes the simplest solutions are the best ones. And so, the TechZone was born in April 1999.

There was no content management system (CMS) back then—refer to Chapter 5: Installing WordPress, for more information on content management systems—so I had to manually add content to the site every day. To help expand the TechZone, I managed to con a couple of local computer stores to loan me hardware to review. A website without quality content isn't going to get anywhere, so this helped a lot. After another month, I decided to try my hand at e-mailing a manufacturer for a product to review. The company that I first contacted was Abit. I asked them for a BH6 motherboard and got no reply. And then a week later, the motherboard showed up at my door! After reviewing the motherboard, I e-mailed them to let them know that I had completed the review, and also to request another motherboard. As before, I got no reply, but, sure enough, the new motherboard arrived about a week later. To this day, Abit has never replied to my requests for review samples, but they have almost always delivered.

Two months after starting the TechZone, I got a call from Ed Homich, who worked for Maximum PC, one of the most respected online magazines in the world of computing. He informed me that he was going to start a network and wanted my site to join. Maximum PC would post my news and sell advertising for my site. Any money made would be split fifty-fifty. I thought, "I can make money doing this?" This was my first exposure to site monetization. Yes, you can make money online!

Being a part of the Maximum PC network was a fun and interesting experience. Unlike other networks, Maximum PC kept their number of affiliates low and they stuck with well-known sites. Some of the original network members include Ars Technica, WinDrivers, and Neoseeker. Ed told me to pump out the content, and he'd send me the traffic. MaximumPC.com was a huge website back then, and they only posted network news.

Interestingly enough, most of the other sites in the Maximum PC network didn't produce very much content. There were times when the Maximum PC home page looked like the TechZone because all the stories on there were from me. This goes to show you that when you feel passionate about something and you're willing to put in the work, the rewards are definitely there for the taking. As I mentioned in the first chapter, you have to make your own opportunities. The other sites in the network just didn't take advantage of this tremendous opportunity in the same way that I did. The first check that I got from Maximum PC was for $250. I remember thinking that this was pretty cool. The next month, the check was for $2,500. That's how fast my traffic was growing.

Networking and Trade Shows

In August of 1999, just four months after launching the TechZone, I got rid of the black background that was so popular in those days. This was based on the recommendation of a site designer. The next month, Ed Homich of Maximum PC gave me another call and he told me that I needed to come to Las Vegas for Comdex. At the time, I'd never heard of it.

Comdex was the biggest technology trade show in North America at the time, attended by over 200,000 people. This not only provided an excellent opportunity to see the latest technological developments, but it was also a fantastic opportunity to do some networking with people who had similar interests. Maximum PC hosted a party and an affiliate awards dinner at Comdex 1999. I received the award for Top Affiliate because I was the fastest growing site in the Maximum PC Network. It's hard to believe that only a few months prior, Moto's Project 504 didn't even exist.

It was also around this time that I decided to register the domain name JohnChow.com. I figured that there had to be millions of John Chows in the world, so I wanted to be the only one to own the domain. After snatching the domain in March 2000, I set up a static home page with a really nifty Flash intro. The fancy animations of Flash helped to give the site a little more personality. Yes, Flash was cool back then, too. The static page basically described who I was and what I did. Here's a brief excerpt:

> *Welcome to the Wired World of John Chow! My name is John Chow (as you no doubt notice from the domain name, hee hee). Right now, the world is under heavy construction. I will update this home page when I have more time (and a better idea of what I want to do with*

it). Running the Wired World keeps me pretty busy (that and hosting the TechZone weekly LAN parties). A little something about myself: I've lived in Vancouver, Canada, pretty much all my life. Before starting the Wired World, I was a partner in a local Richmond printing company. After over a decade of running a print shop, I decided it was time for a change. The Wired World is my attempt at making my stake on the Internet. So far, so good. :)

The Wired World of John Chow even had a guestbook. Remember those things? Even though I said that I would figure out what to do with the home page at some point, that didn't really happen until years later. I even bought the .org and .net extensions at one point, but I never updated them.

Getting back to the TechZone, I gave the site a massive overhaul and a major redesign while the Internet business was still booming. The most important change was the implementation of a real content management system (CMS) and the creation of a true database. Geek-speak aside, what this meant was that I didn't have to manually update the home page each time I wrote new content. The content and the physical layout of the site were managed separately, just as most blogs are handled today with WordPress and similar CMS platforms. This new system made it a lot easier to update the site and contributed a lot to the growth of the TechZone. Things were going great and people were getting very rich from the Web. The Internet money train was chugging along at full speed and I was totally on board. I even turned down an offer of $1.3 million for the TechZone at one point. It looked like the party was going to last forever, but we all know what happened next.

The Dot-Com Crash of 2001

And the dot-com boom went bust. It was during the first few months of 2001 that we saw what would be the beginning of the end of the Internet money train. The United States was going into a recession, and investors finally started to question the sky-high valuation placed on a dot-com business. During this time, it was not out of the question for a dot-com startup to raise $20 million from an IPO (Initial Public Offering: a company's first offer to sell stock publicly), only to spend the entire $20 million to build their brand. The money was spent on advertising and marketing, rather than being spent on research, development, and capital growth. As you can imagine, many of these dot-com startups went bust. Being a media site, the TechZone benefited greatly from that flood of advertising money, and I wasn't shy to drink from that supply every chance that I got. Unfortunately, that well was drying up and drying up fast.

One by one, I watched as all the ad networks that I dealt with go under. This included the Maximum PC network that gave me my first real taste of making money from a website. Many of my fellow website owners also went under during the crash. Some of them were run by really great people, but they just couldn't afford to pay the bills without any money coming in.

It was not a good time to get involved with an online business, and I saw my monthly income drop from $10,000 to just $1,500 during this dark period. Needless to say, this really rained on my parade, and it drastically changed my lifestyle. During the boom days, I was spending over $1,500 a month on just eating out. Naturally, it was not possible to maintain this lifestyle with just $1,500 a month in total income! I managed to survive the dot-com crash because the cost of running my site was pretty small, and I had quite a bit of money saved up from when the sun was still shining. The same can't really be said for a lot of other people who were riding the dot-com wave.

Comdex 2001 was certainly a different experience than Comdex 1999, and this was largely a result of the events of September 11. I remember that I had to go by car because our airline had gone under just two days before Comdex started. Having the trade show take place only two months after 9/11 made for an eerie environment. Security was super tight; we had to go through metal detectors and bag checks before we could even get onto the trade show floor. On the flip side, Comdex also had some of the most amazing parties I have ever attended. I guess everyone just needed some kind of release, and many companies staged huge parties to help us forget our worries, if only for a little while.

Relationships Are Everything

Despite the fact that you may work from home as a professional blogger, it does not mean that you'll be working in a vacuum. The relationships that you develop with other bloggers and online entrepreneurs can mean the world to your potential success. This was certainly the case when the TechZone fell on hard times in 2001. Thankfully, I had some rather terrific relationships.

It was during this time that my sponsors came to my rescue. With all the ad networks dying or dead, the hardware manufacturers stepped up to the plate and bought ad spaces on sites that they were already dealing with. Instead of going through an ad network, websites like the TechZone started dealing with advertisers directly. I still remember chatting over ICQ (an instant messaging program) with Lester of Abit Computer (yes, the same company that never seemed to reply to my requests for hardware review units).

He asked me how much it would cost for a 160x600 pixel ad spot on the TechZone. I gave him the price for one month and he promptly replied, "We'll take a year." It was through deals like these that I managed to slowly build my Internet income to about $4,000 to $5,000 a month. I stayed at that level for most of the bust years. I kept wondering whether the Internet would ever be able to recover and come back to life. Would the Internet money train ever pick up speed and get back on its tracks? Then one day, in the summer of 2003, a little something called Google Adsense joined the party.

Google to the Rescue

Google is the world's most popular search engine, but they also offer a number of other services that are absolutely crucial to the online entrepreneur. I'll go into more detail in later chapters, but there was one very special development in the summer of 2003 that may have single-handedly brought the Internet back to life. If you were to put a date on when the money train pulled back into the station, it would be June 18, 2003. This was the day that Google launched Adsense.

Google Adsense is a program that allows website publishers to serve ads precisely targeted to the specific content of their individual web pages. Contrast this to previous advertising models where the ads would be placed manually, and individual relationships between web publisher and product had to be forged. Before Adsense, I was selling my own advertising to manufacturers that supplied me with review products, like Abit Computer. Under the Adsense system however, *anyone* could make money from a website and they didn't need to make these individual arrangements.

Google Adsense also served as my first experiment with Cost Per Click (CPC) ads. This meant that I would only get paid when a site visitor clicked on the ad. Before this, all of my ads were either on a flat monthly fee or a Cost Per 1000 (CPM) rate. Advertisers simply paid based on the number of page impressions, rather than how effective the ad really was at sending traffic to their respective websites. I wasn't exactly sure what to expect, because the site needed to do more than just show the ads; readers would have to click on the ads, and this created a whole new dynamic altogether.

I was anxious to get started, so I signed up for Google Adsense near the end of June 2003. The first Google-powered ad was served on the TechZone on July 1. Back then, Google only had one ad size: the 468×60 banner, and the colors were fixed. Luckily for me, the default color was blue and this scheme match the recent redesign of The TechZone fourth generation site almost perfectly! This was much more than could be said about some of my friends' sites. As the ad network continued to grow and mature, more color and ad size options would be offered. The train was back.

In my first month with Google Adsense, I only made $371.17. The next month, however, brought a check for $1,106.99. I was really starting to see the potential. As Google added more customization, web publishers could tweak the ads to increase the click rate. Using Adsense was nothing like the CPM banners that I had been using up until then. With CPM banners, all I had to do was slap them up anywhere and be done with it. The money just rolled in. With Google Adsense, I had to adjust the colors, sizes, placement, and integration, because my income was directly dependent on the ad's performance. No clicks, no money.

It was a learning experience, to be sure. To find out how to maximize my profits under the Google Adsense system, I create a series of test sites, so that I could target the highest-paying keywords. I also used these sites to determine which ad units and color schemes produced the best results. It was a lot of experimentation and it continues to be an ongoing learning experience.

Google is largely responsible for the revival of the Web; they made it possible to make money online again. Net advertising was booming again, and by the end of 2004, advertising on the Internet surpassed the peak period achieved in 2000. New ad networks were popping up left and right to capitalize on this monumental growth, and I was once more starting to make some serious money. Things were looking really good, and they continued to be good. The TechZone is now one of the most trusted resources on the Internet, and the advertising opportunities have quickly expanded beyond Adsense. Even so, without Google, the TechZone—and the Web in general—would not be what it is today.

Blogging Hits the Scene

Remember how I said that I bought the JohnChow.com domain way back in March 2000? Remember how I said that the update wouldn't come until years later? Well, it shouldn't really surprise you that the site didn't rank all that well in the search engines, given its complete lack of updates. If someone went into Google and searched for "John Chow," they probably wouldn't be able to find my home page. That's just not acceptable, now is it? I knew that Google placed higher value on sites that were updated more often, so I figured that it would be a good idea to transform the site into a blog.

In November 2005, I finally gave John Chow Dot Com the attention it deserved, and transformed it from a single static page into a full-fledged blog. It launched on December 1, 2005. Let me tell you, the John Chow Dot Com of 2005 was nothing like what it is today. At that time, my primary motivation was to get my spot in the Google results page, and I achieved this goal a lot sooner than I expected. Just *two days* after launching the blog, John Chow Dot Com skyrocketed its way to the number one result in the search results for "John Chow." I expected to get back on the list, to be sure, but I wasn't expecting Google to put me back at the number one spot quite so fast! That probably explains why Google is the world's top search engine.

John Chow Dot Com started out as simply a place to put all the miscellaneous ramblings that didn't belong on the TechZone. I'd write about whatever came to mind, and it just so happened that what came to mind was making money online. Even so, the blog lacked any sort of advertising at the time. The goal wasn't to make money from the blog; I just wanted to ramble. And ramble I did for almost a year, before the blog saw advertising for the first time.

It's Time to Make Money Blogging

In September 2006, I decided that it would be worthwhile to run a case study, to see if a personal blog could make money with Google Adsense. Up until then, most personal blogs on the Internet were not making any money, largely because people didn't think that it was possible. It was expected that a commercial site like the TechZone could make money, but could a personal blog like John Chow Dot Com be as lucrative? Well, in the month of September, my blog made $352.94. Bear in mind that the ads were not turned on until September 17, and the ads were far from being optimized for the site. The $352.94

represented just thirteen days of monetization with un-optimized ads, which works out to $27.15 a day. Not bad for my first attempt!

The following month, I added Vibrant Media IntelliTXT to the mix and came out with a much more impressive figure. The total income generated by John Chow Dot Com in October 2006 was $1,361.64. As the blog continued to grow, the case study got more interesting and diverse. It goes to show you that it is 100 percent possible to make a very healthy income from a personal blog. Today, John Chow Dot Com makes in excess of $30,000 a month, representing an annual income of well over $300,000. What began as a personal platform to express my opinions and views is now a well-respected resource for anyone looking to make money online.

It is important that you not view your blog as a lifeless entity. It is something that must continually evolve, change, and adapt. When John Chow Dot Com was first launched, it made use of a free WordPress theme that was readily available to anyone. When I was ready to take the blog to the next level, I enlisted the services of a professional web designer—Nate Whitehill, from Unique Blog Designs—to come up with a custom WordPress theme, one that was designed to be monetized to the fullest. The new theme was launched in August 2007, and it featured several new advertising opportunities. If it wasn't for the new theme, the blog would not be where it is today.

Learning from History

Some people may say that this history lesson has little relevance to making money on the Internet today. They also say that those who don't study history are doomed to repeat it. We are now in the middle of another dot-com boom. There are literally thousands of blogs on the Internet that are making a sizable income, let alone all the other dot-com start-ups that are garnering all sorts of attention (and money). The Internet is bigger than ever. Take a look at services like Twitter, MySpace, Blogger, YouTube—the list goes on and on. Once again, we're starting to see some crazy valuation placed on unproven concepts.

Facebook has been valued at $15 billion and Microsoft even purchased a 1.6 percent share of the social networking site for $240 million. All I need now is for someone to make me a multi-million dollar offer for the TechZone and the circle will be complete.

It's hard to say whether history is repeating itself and whether or not we're heading for Dot Com Crash 2.0. That said, I'm more prepared than ever because of how much I've learned since discovering the Internet and the ability to make money online. The single greatest lesson that I've learned is simply to keep learning. I hope that this book will serve as a launching pad for your online endeavors and that you'll enjoy the same level of success that I have. You too can make money online. You too can be a dot-com mogul.

Chapter Three:
Blogging 101

In this chapter, you'll learn what a blog is, who will gain the most from reading this book, and three critical tips for the beginning blogger.

When blogs first started popping up on the Internet, the vast majority were personal journals people used to express their individual thoughts and feelings about things. You could say that they were public diaries; they were nowhere near what blogs are today. Sure, there are people who still use their blogs as a diary of sorts, but there are countless other professional blogs on the Internet that are purely out there to make money. Many of the most popular websites today are blogs. People turn to Autoblog for their car news, Kotaku for video game news, Gizmodo for news related to computers and technology, and they turn to John Chow Dot Com to read about the most effective ways to make money online, particularly from blogging. But what is a blog in the first place? If you want to make money from a blog, you must first understand what it is.

At its core, a blog— short for web log—is a specialized website that is frequently updated, usually with entries displayed in reverse chronological order. The actual subject matter varies considerably. Types of blogs include personal blogs, where people write about what they had for lunch, what their kids are doing that day, or what's on their minds; commercial blogs, that talk about the latest news in a variety of industries; celebrity blogs; fan blogs; and all sorts of other types. The key difference between a blog and a conventional website isn't the format—it's the fact that the posts are usually pretty personal, offering personal insights and commentary. For a blog to truly be successful, the posts have to offer an opinion. Readers don't want dry news; they want your perspective. That's what makes a blog special.

A blog can be run by a single individual or by a group of individuals. Many commercial blogs, like Lifehacker, for example, are run by several people; whereas a more personal blog (even one with advertising) will focus on a single individual. Popular personal blogs on making money online and making money from a blog would include Darren Rowse's blog (problogger.net) and Jeremy Schoemaker's blog (shoemoney. com). And of course there's John Chow Dot Com.

Who this Book is For and Who It's Not For

There are people out there who only want to use their blogs for personal expression. This book may not necessarily be for them. On the other hand, if you're looking to grow your readership, expand your exposure, and make as much money as possible from a blog, then this is the book for you. I've always said that if you want to do something, then you should really do it. This definitely applies to the world of blogging as well; because if you're not dedicated to your blog and its growth, it's not going to generate the level of income that you want. It's not going to have the readership that you want. At the same time, if you're looking to monetize your blog, then *really monetize your blog*. There's little point in going about it half-heartedly, deciding to just plop a single Google Adsense unit on your site and be satisfied with the pennies you may end up earning each month. If you want to earn over $30,000 a month from a single blog like I do, then you'll want to take this seriously. But don't forget to have fun too. Life without fun is just not worth it.

This book will prove most useful to people who:
- Are serious about making a livable income from blogging
- Are willing to take risks and try new things
- Are not adverse to placing advertising on their blogs
- Are dedicated to the growth of their blogs
- Are determined never to stop learning
- Have real goals and will develop a plan to achieve those goals
- Want to be successful online

This book may be less useful to people who:
- See blogging as just a hobby
- Are not willing to take a few risks
- Are not willing to put in 110 percent
- Are not interested in having fun

Yes, you must be motivated to make money online, but there is at least one other very critical characteristic that you should have too: passion.

Tip #1: Blog About Your Passion

We all want to be successful: that much is clear. The trouble is that very few people will follow through on their plans all the way to the end because they either get discouraged, or they lose interest along the way. The same is true when it comes to starting and running a successful blog. Some of the best blogs on the Internet are those that approach a certain niche. They're focused, so visitors know exactly what to expect when they come to that blog. For example, readers of John Chow Dot Com know that it's a blog largely about making money online. It's fine to deviate from your niche from time to time, so long as you maintain the main focus of your site. And this main focus, or niche, is of utmost importance.

When choosing the topic for your blog, you should choose very carefully. Unless you plan on packing it in within the first couple of months, you'll want to choose a topic that you'll be willing to stick with over the long haul. Some people love video games, while others like watching the stock market. The key is that you need to choose a topic that you're passionate about. If you're not passionate about the focus of your blog, you're not going to stick with it, and chances are that you'll want to give up after a short while. Needless to say, this is a very unsuccessful proposition. I don't write about making money online because it is a popular or lucrative niche to write about. I write about making money online because I am passionate about the topic. The best way to decide if you're passionate about what you plan to blog about is to ask yourself if you'd be willing to do it for free. If you would, then you have probably found your topic. People who blog only for money seldom succeed: their lack of passion can be felt by the readers (who *are* passionate about the topic).

Go to a cat fancier's blog, for example, and you'll find that most of the visitors are cat owners or cat lovers themselves. If they come to a blog written by someone who hates animals and has no passion about kitties, then the readers won't stick around and the blog will ultimately fail. The posts would lack personal perspective and passion. Blogs attract like-minded individuals and the visitors will see right through you if you're just in it for the money.

If the only reason you're blogging is to get rich, you will fail.

Furthermore, if you are truly passionate about your topic, you will be more motivated to stay up- to-date with the related industry. You're going to be visiting similar websites and blogs in order to find out what's happening in your niche, not because it could be a way for you to make money, but because it's something you want to know about anyway. Your passion for the topic will help you through the rough patches when you may not be making a lot of money or attracting a large number of visitors. Yes, you will want to employ tactics to grow both—I'll get to these in later chapters—but you'll continue to work on your blog because you are passionate about the niche, and your readers will respect you for this.

Tip #2: Get Your Own Domain

After you have decided on your niche, it's probably time for you to find a home for your new blog. You may already be familiar with free blogging platforms available on websites like WordPress.com and Blogger.com. While it is possible to place advertising on a Blogger.com blog, this is not a method I recommend if you're at all interested in making a sizable income from blogging. Instead, I highly recommend that every beginning blogger purchase his or her own domain name. It used to be that owning your own website was restricted to real companies, but this has drastically changed in recent years. The cost of registering your own domain name is next to nothing—only a few dollars a year—but the potential rewards from doing this are monumental.

Even though you may be starting a personal blog, you still want to be viewed as professional. There are countless benefits to having your own domain name. For example, don't you think that people will take you more seriously as a professional blogger if your web address is yourname.com rather than yourname.blogspot.com? The former has a much greater air of professionalism, whereas the latter implies that the blog is only a hobby. Ad networks will also take you a lot more seriously if you have your own domain name, and many ad networks don't even allow WordPress.com and Blogger.com blogs into their fray. You need your own domain name.

But I'm just getting started. I'll get my own domain after I get the hang of this a little better.

This is something I hear from a lot of beginning bloggers. The fact of the matter is that if you take this path, you will ultimately regret it down the line. If you start out with a Blogger.com account, for example, you might work hard to develop backlinks, Alexa rankings, Google PageRank, and all those metrics that are so important to running a successful blog. When you choose to migrate your blog to your own domain, all of those achievements go down the toilet and you'll have to start over again. In contrast, if you start right from the get-go with your own domain, your hard work will quickly accumulate, and you'll get to keep everything you earn.

WordPress is my blogging platform of choice. Be aware that the WordPress platform is not exactly the same thing as WordPress.com! In order to use the real WordPress content management system, you'll need to get some web hosting. I recommend that you go with BlueFur. com (they host my blog). If you use JohnChowRocks in the coupon code area, they'll give you 15 percent off. It costs less than $10 a month for the basic hosting package, and if you do things correctly, you will easily recoup this cost through the money your blog generates. If you can't make $10 a month from blogging, you've still got a lot to learn. Using the self-hosted WordPress platform offers a lot more flexibility.

Tip #3: Update Often

Remember when I defined a blog at the beginning of this chapter? I said that a blog is a specialized website that is *updated frequently*. This is very important to the success of a blog. Unfortunately, it seems that most bloggers don't understand this concept. Inevitably, countless people hear about how easy it is (or so it sounds) to make money from blogging, so they get all excited about it. They seem very passionate about their niche, and they even manage to register an appropriate domain name. They're off to a good start, right? When the blog goes live, they put up a flurry of posts in the first few days, and this excitement really comes through. They think they're doing great, and they might even keep up this posting schedule for the first few weeks.

And then the number of posts starts to decrease, and eventually, the blog is hardly updated at all. These kinds of bloggers come flying out the gate, but they exhaust themselves almost immediately. They lose interest and enthusiasm when they see that they're not attracting as many readers as they had hoped. They log into their Google Adsense account to discover that they have only earned three cents in the last week. Disappointed and discouraged, they basically give up on their blog. They point toward the steadily decreasing level of traffic and say that no matter what they do, they seem to be doomed to failure.

Guess what? They have no one to blame but themselves.

Nothing kills a blog faster than a lack of updates. If you're going to start a blog, then you should choose a posting frequency that you are able to maintain over the long run. Choose how often you're going to update your blog, and then stick to this schedule. If you're not able to commit to a set schedule, you might not be ready to make money blogging. A blog has to be updated on a regular basis and a nonupdated blog is a dead blog. Ideally, you want to have a new post each and every day, but if you're not comfortable with this, then start out slower. It's better to have one post per week, every week, than to have five posts in one day and then nothing for the next month.

Chapter Four:
Ten Essential Blogging Tips

In this chapter, you'll learn ten of the most important things that any professional blogger should know, and what you should do if you want to be truly successful.

There's more to making money from a blog than just throwing up some content, slapping on a few ads, and waiting for the money to start rolling in. Whether this is your first time running a blog, or you're already a veteran of getting of your opinion out there in the most effective manner, these ten tips will get you that much closer to becoming a blogging superstar.

1. Be Personal

When readers come to your blog, they're not expecting you to just report the news. The whole point of a blog is that it isn't CNN or News. com. People read blogs to see your unique opinion and perspective. Your should write every post from your point of view, letting your readers know exactly how you feel about whatever it is that you are blogging about that day.

Did you hear about the unveiling of a new sports car? Don't just report on all the specifications and how much horsepower the engine happens to generate. Tell you readers *why* you are interested in this vehicle and how you think it compares to other sports cars in its class. Your opinion counts more than you think. People don't watch *The Colbert Report* to find out the latest in the world of politics; they watch *The Colbert Report* because of Stephen Colbert's unique perspective on what is happening in the world. Your blog should be no different! Without personality, your blog is just regurgitating what can easily be found elsewhere. The most unique thing about your blog is *you*. Don't ever forget that.

Is your blog unique? I am certainly not the first person to write about making money online, and I most definitely won't be the last. With literally thousands of other similar blogs on the Web, what makes John Chow Dot Com so special? While I offer a lot of original ideas in many of my blog posts, like some of the evil marketing techniques that I like to deploy, I also write a lot about things that other people are talking about, too. The difference is I add my own views to make each post unique. One of the worst things you can do is just copy and paste text from another blog. Use another post as a springboard, sure, but you have to offer your own personality to each post too. Be unique. Be personal.

2. Write for Your Readers, Not for the Search Engines

Google and other search engines may be a vital source of traffic for your blog, but it is ultimately *people* who read what you're writing! It isn't wrong to be mindful of things like keyword density (how often a certain keyword, like "sports cars," appears in an article), but you should ultimately write in a way that is easily understood by your readers. I'm sure you've come across articles on the Internet that were clearly written with search engine optimization in mind. The net result is a piece that is completely incoherent, and even though the author has done everything in his power to make it search engine friendly, Google will tend to ignore it because Google follows people. And people don't like reading incoherent garbage.

If you want to successfully make money from a blog, you need to think of your readers, and think about how you can grow your audience. Write in a way that gets your point across clearly. If what you're writing is good, the traffic will follow even if it's not perfectly optimized for Google or any other search engine.

3. Get to Know Your Readers

Although it may appear otherwise, blogging is not a one-way form of communication. Readers are not passive individuals who are just sitting there, absorbing what you have to say. They can instantly voice their opinions right back at you, either via a comment form or by writing a post on their own blogs. The beauty of a blog is that the blogger is so accessible to his or her readers. Contrast this to a television show or traditional newspaper, where the audience is quite separate from the person creating the content. By getting to know your readers—their preferences, and their expectations—you can better serve the community, and this will ultimately show up in your bottom line.

The most successful bloggers are those that interact with their readers. They look for feedback and constructive criticism. They open the lines of communication by replying to e-mails in a timely manner and by responding to questions posted in the comments. When you interact with your readers in this way, it builds trust and loyalty. You appear more approachable, and you actually appear human! It's important to connect on a personal level, because networking with other bloggers can be the best thing you can do for your own blog.

4. Never Rush Your Posts

In the previous chapter, I talked about the importance of updating your blog often and on a regular basis. I also said that it is ideal if you can write a new blog post at least every day. Well, the trouble with trying to keep up with a posting schedule like this is that you can sometimes feel pressured to complete a blog post within a very short time frame. Maybe you need to finish writing it before dinner, because otherwise you won't have another opportunity to get a post up today. You know what? It doesn't matter. You should never rush your posts. Your readers will be able to see right through your haste because the post will feel unpolished, and it will likely contain a whole bunch of grammatical mistakes. Not good.

Most bloggers fall victim to the rushed post syndrome from time to time, possibly because a hot story comes up, and you want to be one of the first bloggers on the Web to talk about it, offering your unique perspective. Always take the time to proofread your posts. Double, even triple-check each post to make sure that it's free of errors. I tend to read over a post three to six times before giving it another grammar check through Microsoft Word. Only then do I hit the Publish button. It's handy to write your posts in a web browser, like Mozilla Firefox, because some of them come with a built-in spell checker. Every word that is spelled incorrectly will be underlined in red. Even so, you shouldn't rely on this tool alone to catch mistakes: the red underline won't show up for a grammatical error or missing punctuation.

5. Go with the Flow

More important than perfect grammar and spelling is the ability to get your point across. You should really focus on the flow of the article. Present your ideas in a seamless fashion, with one paragraph following another in an understandable and logical manner. The best way to achieve this is to try and write each blog post in one sitting. It is often better to let the ideas come pouring out, and then revisit the post later to remove the unnecessary fluff, and delete the redundant words.

If your article seems to be jumping back and forth between seemingly unrelated thoughts, your readers will get confused. Think of each blog post as a short story or a television show. These forms of entertainment wouldn't make sense if the action jumped all over the place and the viewer wasn't introduced to the characters. Readers won't return to your blog if reading it is a frustrating experience.

When you have trouble putting together a fluid blog post, it can sometimes be helpful to construct a brief outline before you start writing, just like you did back in school for your essays. I know, I know. You don't want to think back to your school days, but the brief outline can be a great strategy for organizing your thoughts. Even if you use this method, I still recommend that you write your post in order, from beginning to end. This will help it to sound like one continuous thought. When you write the sections out of order, you'll lose the flow.

6. Read Other Blogs

Blogging doesn't exist in a vacuum. It's not just you sitting in front of the computer, pumping out the content each day, and hoping for the money to start rolling in. Just as it is important to interact with your readers, you should also go out and read other blogs, particularly those in your niche. This serves several purposes. It exposes you to different writing styles, which can help to improve your own writing ability. Also, you can see how other people piece their articles together and present their ideas. You don't want to be a copycat, but you can certainly take inspiration from other bloggers.

By reading other blogs, you are also able to keep up with the latest news in your niche. These are items that you may not have heard otherwise. Better still, these posts can serve as a launching pad for a blog post of your own, because as I mentioned earlier, you can report on things that have already been covered on the Web, as long as you offer your own personal opinion and perspective on the issue. Don't forget that your readers read your blog for *your* opinion. While you're at it, don't forget to link to other blogs in your niche too. If you want to get backlinks from other blogs (this helps with traffic development and getting your site ranked in popular search engines), you also have to be willing to dole out the link love too. The most successful bloggers don't hoard their links. Say *hi* to other blogs in your niche and they just might say *hi* back.

Another major advantage that you can enjoy from reading other blogs in your niche is the opportunity to network with like-minded individuals. This is why it's important that you not only read other blogs in your niche, but also leave comments. If it wasn't for Michael Kwan's many comments on John Chow Dot Com, I wouldn't have known who he was, and he wouldn't be working with me today. This demonstrates the social aspect of blogging.

This is also why you should make it as easy as possible for people to leave comments on your blog. There are some sites out there that force users to register before they are able to leave a comment. The extra speed bump is often enough to deter casual readers from commenting, and, lest you forget, casual readers can eventually become loyal readers! Let them comment. If you're concerned about spam, there are plenty of solutions for that too, which I will address in a later chapter.

7. Don't Let the Haters Get To You

It's impossible to please everyone. We all know this on an intellectual level, but it can be pretty disheartening when you find a negative comment on your blog. Some of these comments go beyond disagreeing with your view, and they can actually get pretty hateful. You know what, though? I actually look forward to getting negative comments on my blog; I'll tell you why. Negative comments are an indication of growth. As your blog gets bigger and attracts more attention, it will necessarily attract a proportionate number of people who hate your guts. This is a good thing!

If you're not getting negative comments, it could mean that you're doing something wrong. This isn't to say that you should go around pissing people off on purpose, but it's impossible to please everyone all the time, and you shouldn't even try. Remember: the most unique thing about your blog is *you*. Don't be afraid to express your honest opinion. Just know that with every voiced opinion, there will be people who agree with you and people who don't. It's important that you don't start a false sense of controversy for the sole purpose of attracting attention to yourself. While this may work in the short run, your readers will eventually see right through it. A lack of trust can harm your blog much more than a few negative comments.

The best part about getting negative comments is that it can spark a great debate on your blog. It encourages discussion, because the differing opinions will battle it out in the comments section. This has the potential to generate a huge level of traffic, and increased traffic gives you a much better opportunity to rake in the cash. It's ironic, really, because the people who say your site's traffic will suffer from your misaligned opinions are the very people who will help you to increase traffic.

Speaking for myself, John Chow Dot Com gets more than its fair share of haters. There are people who say the site has sold out, or lost its value. There are people who say there's too much advertising on the site and that this can only hurt my numbers. These same people are the ones who say that they will never come back… but they always do. You'll know that you've gone too far when the traffic drops. If your traffic is still growing, it means that you are doing something right, regardless of what the most vocal minority may say to the contrary.

8. Use the Art of the Deep Link

A regular link is when you link to a top-level domain, like http://www. johnchow.com. A deep link is a link to a specific article within the top-level domain. From Google's point of view, a deep link is just as, if not more, important because it shows the search engine exactly what content within a particular website is the most relevant and the most popular. When you are writing a blog post, try to deeplink some of your older articles. This not only tells Google a little more about each individual page, but it can also direct readers to content that they may not have seen before. Additionally, it helps Google to discover articles that it may have missed.

You shouldn't force it, of course, but you should deeplink to older posts whenever they are relevant to your current post. Even if they are not perfectly relevant, there is always a way to find a connection between something you had written in the past and the post that you are writing now. Another thing that you should remember is that when you are deeplinking to yourself (or others, for that matter), you should avoid using vague anchor text like "click here." Instead, you should always use a descriptive anchor text because this helps the search engines better understand what the target article is about. The user experience is better too.

One final reason why you should always deeplink to your articles is that there are "scrapers" on the Web that will steal your content, usually from your RSS feed. These scrapers are usually pretty lazy, though, and rip entire posts with all the links intact. You will then see these trackbacks and pingbacks in your blogging dashboard, informing you of which sites are stealing your content. At worst, you get a bunch of links back to your blog, which could lead to a few more visitors.

9. Offer a Full Feed RSS

RSS stands for really simple syndication and it is a way that readers are able to subscribe to your blog. These updates can then be accessed through a feed aggregator—like Google Reader—or you can also offer subscription via e-mail. In both cases, it is in your best interest to offer a full feed (which contains entire posts) instead of a partial feed (which only contains a brief snippet). Many RSS users simply will not subscribe to a feed unless it is a full feed. Speaking for myself, I have over 30 feeds in my Google Reader and every single one of them is a full feed. I simply cannot be bothered with partial feeds, because it almost eliminates the utility of subscribing in the first place.

It is true that the RSS feed is mostly ad-free and it can be more difficult to make money from it, but it is ultimately more important to develop a strong following of readers. With more readers comes more exposure. With more exposure comes more traffic. And with more traffic comes a heck of a lot more money. One of the worst mistakes you can make is using a partial feed as a teaser for your readers, hoping that they will click through to read the full article on your blog. All this does is frustrate readers, and many of them will ultimately unsubscribe. Unless your blog is updated over 20 times a day, it's unlikely that readers would be willing to put up with a partial feed.

10. Take Advantage of the Ramp

A technical term found mostly in manufacturing, the ramp describes the process of going from zero to full output. When a new product is launched, for example, the company wants to get production up to maximum capacity as soon as possible. The same can be said about trying to make money by blogging. You don't have to hit the ramp right from the beginning, but the only way that you will ever make it onto the A-list is if you take advantage of the ramp. Traffic is not built on a linear scale. It grows in leaps and bounds, and the sooner you hit the ramp, the better off you will be.

The best way to increase exposure to your blog is not through slow and steady growth. It is more effective to make a concentrated promotional effort some time during your blog's life. Instead of spending $100 a month into promotion for a year, it is a much better strategy to spend $1,000 in one month, and then $10 a month for the rest of the year. Bombard the Web with several promotional efforts all at the same time. Several companies and blogs have used paid reviews on John Chow Dot Com as part of their ramp attempt. The ones that have done the best are the ones that combined the review with several other simultaneous marketing strategies.

John Chow Dot Com hit the Ramp when I experienced thirty front page Diggs (getting on the front page of http://digg.com/ can bring a huge boost in traffic) in less than three months. You don't have to spend a lot of money to ramp up traffic to your blog, but it's probably the easiest way to do it. If you don't have the cash, feel free to get creative! The blogosphere loves uniqueness!

Chapter Five:
WordPress Basics

In this chapter, you'll learn about how to install WordPress and five critical elements to a successful blog.

A sk many of the top bloggers on the Internet to name their preferred blogging software, and an overwhelming majority will tell you that they use WordPress. There are other options out there like Movable Type, but there are several reasons why WordPress is so popular. For starters, it is 100% free for download from http://wordpress.org/. You certainly can't beat the price of free. Even though it goes for zero dollars, the blogging platform is feature-rich and incredibly user-friendly. The website also includes installation instructions. For people who are already familiar with things like mySQL databases and FTP uploads, the process will be an absolute cinch, and can be completed in less than five minutes.

For people who are not as savvy with web-based tools, WordPress.org also offers a volunteer-run service that will install the popular blogging platform for you. Even so, I recommend that you go through the process yourself because understanding how WordPress works will ultimately help you in your journey towards making money from blogging. If the web-hosting company of your choosing happens to support it, an even easier way to install WordPress is through Fantastico, a preloaded software package. For example, the company that hosts John Chow Dot Com—BlueFur.com—fully supports Fantastico. If your web host does support it, then you can use Fantastico to install WordPress. It only takes a few clicks, and the entire thing can be done in about a minute or two.

After WordPress has been installed, it's time to start making that blog your own. There is no way that you will ever make any money using the default WordPress template, especially if you don't customize it at all. The following are five critical areas that you should consider when starting your money-making blog.

Unique Blog Theme

Quality content will ultimately be the biggest reason why people will want to come back to your blog, but at the same time, you don't want to present that awesome material in the most generic of fashions. As much as we would like to hope otherwise, appearances mean a lot, whether it be when you meet a business associate in person, or when a visitor finds his or her way onto your website. We've all come across websites with nasty flashing banners in every direction, or poor navigation. Even if the content of this site is valuable, Web users will not return if the usability and feel of the site is not up to snuff.

Some people call them templates, other people call them themes. Whatever you want to call them, WordPress themes will define the overall look of your blog. It is through the theme that you can define things like the color scheme, the number and orientation of the sidebars, the placement of the navigational links, and so forth. When I first started John Chow Dot Com, I made use of one of the many free WordPress themes available on the Internet: Mistylook. As the blog matured and when I was ready to take the blog to the next level, I elicited the services of a professional blog designer to come up with a custom WordPress template, one that was optimized from the beginning to maximize advertising revenues. If you really want to take making money from a blog seriously, you will need a custom theme at some point, though when you choose to take this step is up to you.

Even if you opt for one of the free themes available on the Web, you'll definitely want to tweak it in several places so that your blog doesn't look exactly like the other blogs using the same theme. You might want to customize the content in the sidebar, adjust the color scheme, and move some other things around. This will require a little bit of coding knowledge, but the blogging community is usually pretty open about providing advice on this front. Having a basic working knowledge of HTML, PHP, and CSS (different web coding languages that are typically used by blogs) will go a long way in helping you to create a unique blog theme. Otherwise, you can just pay a web designer to do it for you.

Unique Header Image

The single greatest thing you can do to make your blog stand out from the crowd also happens to be one of the easiest. You absolutely *have to* have a unique header image. There is nothing less professional than coming to a blog that only has plain text in the top banner because it shows that the owner didn't even bother going through the trouble of personalizing the blog. If you're already an artist of sorts, it's very easy to throw together a custom header image, and many of the newer WordPress themes come with an easy, menu-style navigation bar for updating your header image. No PHP required!

The header image should be something that is distinctive to your blog, expresses your personality, and says a little something about what visitors should expect when they start to browse around on your website. Speaking for myself, the first header image for John Chow Dot Com featured a Chevy Corvette. Outside of making money online, one of my major interests is fast cars. The Corvette also symbolized one of the big goals of trying to make money online: being able to afford a fast car. As the blog matured, I swapped out the Corvette for a pair of Pagani Zonda F's, because they are better-looking and more unique. Just like me. When I got a complete blog makeover, I once again changed the header image to a Lamborghini Reventon.

Other popular blogs on the Internet make use of distinctive fonts, interesting logos, and even some personal caricatures! What you do with the header image on your blog is totally up to you, but the most important thing is to make it unique. This will help to establish your brand. Think about some of the best-known logos on the planet—Apple Computer, Motorola, Intel, etc.—and they are all instantaneously recognizable by anyone who sees them. The same should be true about your blog.

Prominently Featured RSS Feed

It appears that people who subscribe to your blog are also the least likely to click on ads. At the same time, without a loyal readership, your blog isn't going to go anywhere. It's always in your best interest to attract as many subscribers as you can, because it means that these people will continue to come back to your blog, read your content, leave comments, and tell their friends about your blog. This obviously has a huge effect on your traffic numbers, and without traffic your blog isn't going to make any money at all. Building a strong readership and developing your traffic should be a top priority, especially when your blog is just starting out.

The more tech-savvy readers will instantly recognize the characteristic orange logo that signifies an RSS feed. For those of you who aren't as familiar, RSS, or Really Simple Syndication, is a way for people to subscribe to a site so that they automatically receive a notification every time the site is updated. Most people use services like Google Reader to manage their RSS subscriptions.

In order to attract RSS subscribers, you want to make it obvious to your readers that you have an RSS feed to begin with. I recommend that you stick with the standard RSS logo because it's distinctive and easily recognizable. Some blogs choose to adjust the color of the logo to better fit with the site's overall design, but that can cause the logo to blend in a little too well. Visitors looking for the button will miss it and, as a result, you'll lose an opportunity to gain another reader.

Be sure to feature your RSS feed as prominently as possible, with the button clearly displayed so that readers won't have to scroll to find it.

If it wasn't for this and other marketing techniques that I employ, John Chow Dot Com would not have reached the level of popularity that it enjoys today. My blog has well over 20,000 subscribers (and counting). They provide a steady flow of traffic to the blog, which translates into higher prices for advertising on my site. As you can imagine, advertisers are willing to pay more money for a placement on a site with one million page views a day than they re for a site that with only one hundred page views a day.

With Feedburner, you are also able to display your current number of subscribers. You should not display this widget until you have a sizable readership. The reason for this is that people are lemmings. They're followers. If they arrive at a blog and see a reader count of five, they'll figure that the blog isn't worth reading. In contrast, when they come to John Chow Dot Com and see the twenty thousand plus readers, they'll assume that there's something of substance and interest here. And there is, of course.

Custom Favicon

What's a favicon? I know that's a question that a lot of people may have because it's not really a common term. In a nutshell, a favicon is a small image file that can be associated with your site or blog. This small image shows up in several places. For instance, you'll notice that when you go to google.com, the little icon at the beginning of the address bar in your browser will likely display the Google "G" logo. When you go to John Chow Dot Com, you'll find a very small picture of me next to the address bar as well. Moreover, when people save a particular website to their favorites, the favicon is usually saved as well, and is displayed next to the name of the site in the bookmarks toolbar.

Well, this favicon isn't automatic. It's not like Firefox or Internet Explorer automatically chooses an image to use for the favicon. In fact, the vast majority of sites on the Internet lack favicons; you can use this to your advantage. Favicons are one way to make your blog stand out in the bookmarks and, implemented correctly, it can also be seen viewed within RSS feed aggregators. There are very specific requirements for favicons, so let me get to those now. Thankfully, it's a very straightforward process.

What you'll want to do is open up your favorite image editing software. While PhotoShop and similar programs are ideal, you can get away with using MS Paint if that's all you have. From there, you'll want to make a very small GIF or PNG image that measures 16 pixels wide and 16 pixels tall. The key is to save the image as favicon.ico. Note that the file extension is .ico (for icon), and not .gif or .png. Make sure you have this component correct, because countless users get confused and end up with files named favicon.ico.gif.

After you have saved the file, you'll want to upload the favicon.ico file to your site's root directory. This is achieved by using an FTP program, much like the one you used to install WordPress and its plug-ins. Normally, this would be enough to make the icon appear next to the browser's address line, but there sometimes are issues with this implementation. To be absolutely certain, you can add the following code in between the <head> tags in your WordPress header.php file. It doesn't really matter where you put it, so long as it is between the <head> and </head> tags.
<link rel="shortcut icon" href="http://www.johnchow.com/favicon.ico">
<link rel="icon" href="http://www.johnchow.com/favicon.ico">

Obviously, you'll want to replace "johnchow.com" with your own domain. And that's all there is to it. Alternatively, you can look into the MaxBlogPress Favicon WordPress plug-in, which automates the creation of a favicon a little more than the manual method. The best feature of this plug-in is that you can upload just about any image file, regardless of file extension (JPG, GIF, PNG, etc.), and it will automatically resize and rename the file accordingly.

Search Engine Optimized URLs

Remember how I said that you should write for people and not for search engines? This is 100 percent true, and if you write solely for search engine optimization (SEO) purposes, your blog won't get anywhere. This is because no one is going to want to read the rubbish you're pumping out for search engine crawlers. Even so, there are several strategies that you can take to improve the SEO of your blog posts without detracting from the user experience. In fact, this following tip can improve both the user experience *and* your search engine ranking in Google.

When you first install WordPress, it will have all the default settings. This includes the default WordPress theme described earlier in this chapter. Another one of the default settings determines how the URLs are set up for each individual blog post. When you write a new blog post, WordPress will generate a dynamic URL based on a sequential number. If your most recent post was number 700, for example, the next blog post will be number 701. More specifically, the link for each post will look something like this: http://www.johnchow.com/?p=701.

This makes logical sense, but it's horrible for search engine optimization. What some people don't know is that Google not only looks at the domain, incoming links, and the actual content of a page to determine its subject matter, but there is also a certain amount of weight placed on what is shown in the URL. In this instance, Google is able to know that the post is in the johnchow.com domain, but it can only guess that the content is about the number "4030." Utter nonsense, right?

Well, wouldn't it be easier if Google could gain a pretty accurate idea about the content of a post even before its spiders crawl the words? You can accomplish this in WordPress by turning on a more SEO-friendly URL. This is much better than the dynamic one displayed above. For example, you can create a URL that looks something like this: http://www.johnchow.com/why-you-need-a-holding-company.

That's a heck of a lot more accurate, right? To activate this URL structure, go to the Options section in your WordPress control panel (e.g., http://www.yourblog.com/wp-admin). From there, click on Permalinks. Displayed on this page are four different permalink structures: default, date and name base, numeric, and custom. The date and name base and the custom permalinks are the best options, because they include the title of the post in the link, as shown above. Some people prefer to have the date attached to the URL, which would look something like this:

http://www.johnchow.com/2008/03/24/why-you-need-a-holding-company.

I personally prefer that the URL *not* include the date, but that's up to you. In order to have just the title, you can use the custom structure /%postname%/.

Chapter Six:
WordPress Techniques and Tools

In this chapter, we'll expand on some of the concepts mentioned in chapter 5, describing some of the best WordPress tweaks and plug-ins.

Now that you've taken care of some of the basics, like creating a custom header image, and optimizing your permalinks for search engine purposes, it's time to move on to some more advanced techniques and some great (free) WordPress plug-ins. These alterations serve several purposes. Some are meant to help your blog rank better in search engines, optimizing how the Google spiders view your site. Others are meant to improve the user experience, helping you to increase the number of readers and visitors to your blog. Others still are just there to make your life a little easier, streamlining the blogging process so you don't get caught up wasting your time on the little things.

The Power of the Timestamp

A common mistake that many beginning bloggers make is publishing their posts the moment they finish writing them. This not only brings up the concerns about proofreading and proper editing mentioned earlier, but the time that you finish writing a post might not be the best time for you to publish it. What can you do to rectify this situation? Well, WordPress has a very handy feature that lets you post-date articles and determine the exact time that your posts will go live. This is particularly handy if you want to write more than one post each day, as is the case with John Chow Dot Com, because it's not good to have all your posts bunched together within a window of an hour or two. It's much more effective, in terms of both user experience and generating traffic, to spread these posts out evenly throughout the day.

The feature that I'm talking about is the Post Timestamp. When you use the writing tool in WordPress, you'll notice that there is a series of widgets placed along the right side. These are used for customizing your posts—specifying which categories to associate with a post, choosing whether or not to allow comments for this particular post, and so forth. One of these options will read "Post Timestamp."

Normally, a post goes live the moment you hit the publish button, but if you edit the contents of the Post Timestamp widget, you can determine exactly when the post will go live. In this way, it is possible to take advantage of your most prolific periods, writing as many blog posts in advance as you can, and then post-timestamp them into the future. This is particularly handy when you know you will be without Internet access for a period of time. For example, if you're taking a flight across the country and won't be able to access your blog during that time, you might want to write your post before the flight and post-timestamp it with a time that occurs while you're in transit. Taking it even further, if you choose to take a few days off, you don't want your blog to lack updates during that time, right? Well, why not write and post-timestamp enough posts to fill your blog during your absence, spreading them out as though you were actually publishing them live?

Another reason why you may want to use the timestamp feature is to be able to publish a post at the most optimal time. For example, if you notice that most people read your blog around noon, it would be good if these visitors had some new content to read at that time. In this way, you might want to time your posts so that they are always published around 9 AM. This is just an example; choosing an optimal time will depend on the traffic patterns of your blog. Don't forget to take international visitors into account as well. What may be the middle of the night for you is the middle of the workday for someone on the other side of the planet.

Using the timestamp feature is incredibly easy, but it could be one of the most useful features in WordPress. If you have never used the timestamp feature in WordPress, I highly recommend it. I make use of it all the time when I travel, and I usually have at least a couple of posts in the queue at any given time. This keeps up a constant flow of content for my readers. Remember: a nonupdated blog is a dead blog.

Setting the Preferred Domain

Contrary to popular belief, there is a difference between www.johnchow. com and johnchow.com. It is true that most websites can be accessed using either of these addresses, but the www prefix actually works in the same way as any other subdomain. For example, Michael Kwan has his blog at btr.michaelkwan.com, but his freelance writing business at www.michaelkwan.com. Most people might not give this a second thought, because they don't care whether a visitor arrives via the www route or via the route that lacks the www prefix. From a search engine optimization standpoint, however, you'll want to define only one route to your blog.

The main reason for this is that Google might punish you for having duplicate content. This is because the content of http://www. example.com/blog-post is the same as what can be found at http:// example.com/blog-post. The difference is subtle, but to Google, these are two separate web pages, just as a blog post on your site is separate from a blog post on my site. Furthermore, having multiple domains means that Google will assign separate PageRanks for the two URLs, even though they point to the exact same page. You've created your own competition!

The easiest way to overcome this problem is to log into your Google Webmaster Tools account, located at http://www.google.com/ webmasters/tools. From there, you can set what is called a preferred domain. The preferred domain is the one that you would like Google to use when the search engine indexes the pages on your website. Sometimes, the preferred domain is also known as the canonical domain. By setting the preferred domain, you help Google to better understand your website. This will also help to more accurately determine PageRank for your blog, which will help you rank better in search engine results. Setting your preferred domain in Google Webmaster Tools is the first half of the equation.

The second half of the equation is ensuring that all site visitors end up viewing your site using the same domain. To do this, you'll need to add what is called a 301 redirect. What you will want to do is edit the .htaccess file in your blog's root directory. If you do not already have a .htaccess file, then you can create one and upload it using a FTP program. For my blog, I would prefer that everyone access the site using http://www.johnchow.com rather than the version that does not have www. To do this, I include the following code in my site's .htaccess file:

```
RewriteEngine On
RewriteCond %{HTTP_HOST} !^(.*)\.johnchow\.com$ [NC]
RewriteRule ^(.*)$ http://www.johnchow.com/$1 [R=301,L]
```

Naturally, you'll need to replace johnchow.com in the second and third lines with your own domain. I should also note that this code will only work with Linux servers with the Apache mod-rewrite module enabled. If that sounds like total gibberish to you, then you should send a message to the support people at your web-hosting company and ask them about it.

What the above code does is redirect all traffic from johnchow.com to www.johnchow.com. This ensures uniformity in user experience and helps to ensure that people linking to my posts will use the appropriate URL. This linking consistency ensures that you are receiving the optimal amount of "link juice" being given to you by other bloggers and website owners. As you can imagine, you could have ten links pointing to one post with www in the address and another ten links pointing to the same post without www in the address. This is distinctly different than having all twenty links point to exactly the same URL.

Fighting Spam Comments with Akismet and More

Spam. It's one of those problems that people have just learned to live with when it comes to anything Internet-related. There's a good chance that you have some sort of spam filter in place with your e-mail program because you'd otherwise get bombarded by countless offers of receiving millions of dollars from some exiled prince, offers of great deals on male "enhancement" medications, and something about a hot girl in your area anxiously awaiting your phone call. The same is true when it comes to running your blog because you will inevitably end up with mounds of spam comments, especially if your blog becomes as popular as John Chow Dot Com.

For instance, my blog gets over five hundred spam comments each and every day. Can you imagine having to delete each comment manually? The horrible thing about comment spam is that the content automatically gets associated with your website, whether you like it or not. Left untouched, some of these comments can show up in search engines and it will look like content that you created yourself! Unless you're peddling Viagra and pornography websites, this is probably not in your best interest.

Thankfully, every installation of WordPress comes preloaded with the Akismet comment spam killer plug-in. In order to use Akismet, you'll need to get an API key, but this is 100 percent free, and the instructions can be found under the Akismet options in your WordPress control panel. To turn on Akismet, all you have to do is go to the plug-ins section of your WordPress control panel and activate it. From there, you can go to the options area and enter your API key. The key can be acquired by getting a free WordPress account. The process is painless, and it will save you hours (not to mention saving your sanity) in the long run.

In addition to Akismet, you may want to look into some other spam-killing WordPress plug-ins and solutions. For example, some blogs automatically send comments containing more than one link to the moderation queue. Blogs that combat spam more aggressively might place comments from all first-time visitors in the moderation queue. This strategy might work when you have a relatively small audience, but if you have a blog with several thousand subscribers, you might end up spending far too much time dealing with the moderation queue if you do this! Also, if you do choose to moderate your comments, you should inform your readers of this.

Look for this code in your comments.php file:

```
<p>
<input name="submit" type="submit" tabindex="5" value="<?php
_e("Say it!"); ?>" />
</p>
```

And replace it with this:

```
<p>
<blockquote>
Comment moderation is in use. Please do not submit your comment
twice -- it will appear shortly.
</blockquote>
<input name="submit" type="submit" tabindex="5" value="<?php
_e("Say it!");?>" />
</p>
```

This reduces any frustration on the part of the commenter because they expect their comments to appear immediately. This notice tells them why their comment is not showing up.

AdSense Deluxe WordPress Plug-In

While I highly recommend that you do not rely solely on Google AdSense to make money from your blog, there's a good chance that you will be using Google's advertising platform at least in the beginning. Even if you don't, this plug-in can be very handy for managing a lot of the advertising you have on your site, particularly the advertising that embed within each post. For example, I include a 300×250 pixel ad box in each and every blog post, which I embed near the top of the post, aligning to the right, and wrapping the text around it. I have found that this is one of the most effective ad placements for my blog (and many other blogs), but it may not necessarily be the best for you. Either way, you should experiment with your ad placements to find the one that is the most lucrative.

While you could include the actual AdSense code in every post, wouldn't it be easier if there were a shortcut? The AdSense Deluxe WordPress plug-in provides exactly that shortcut. All you need to do is enter the code into the AdSense Deluxe options area. The code that's saved as the default can then be integrated into a post using the code <!--adsense-->. If you have multiple codes entered into the AdSense Deluxe options, each of these can carry a unique name and can be called upon by using this unique name. For example, if you saved one as "banner," then you would call upon that code in a post by typing <!--adsense#banner-->. If you can't remember all of these, you'll notice that all the ad placements will be available through a pull-down menu in the WordPress Write tool. These become available after you've saved your post (use "Save and Continue") at least once.

The other cool thing about AdSense Deluxe is that it keeps track of the number of Google ads displayed and limits that number to three. This is the maximum number of ads allows on a page. It's an easy way to stick to Google's rules and maximize your AdSense profit. Better still, it means that if you ever update the code, you don't need to go through each and every blog post to change it. All you have to do is go into the options area for AdSense Deluxe and edit it once. It will automatically update each post that included the code.

Feedburner FeedSmith

There are several ways that a reader may be able to access your RSS feed. It is in your best interest to aggregate all of these methods into a single consolidated feed. This way, you can have the most accurate representation of your audience size. Feedburner is a popular service for exactly this purpose, and it comes with all sorts of extras that a regular feed would not offer. For example, Feedburner allows you to keep track of exactly how many people are subscribed to your blog. It also provides an easy way for you to offer e-mail subscriptions on your blog. E-mail subscriptions are a great tool because not everyone makes use of RSS aggregators like Google Reader.

Furthermore, you'll want to install the Feedburner FeedSmith WordPress plug-in. It grabs all the different methods of subscribing to your blog and aggregates them into the Feedburner service. For example, people might be able to access your blog's RSS feed by each of the following ways:

http://www.example.com/feed/

http://www.example.com/rss/

http://www.feedburner.com/wp-rss2.php

There are countless other variations that may pop up. By using the Feedburner FeedSmith plug-in, all RSS feeds to your blog are automatically directed to the Feedburner path. This ensures accurate readership statistics, and it automatically converts any existing subscribers from the old feed to the Feedburner one.

Some other useful things about Feedburner: you can create a widget showing how many people accessed your feed yesterday, it can show you how people are subscribing to your blog (which reader they are using), and it can provide a history of the number of subscribers. This last feature is for *all time*, so you can track the growth of your blog. There are all sorts of other features as well, so be sure to check out everything that Feedburner has to offer.

Subscribe to Comments

I encourage people to comment on my blog, whether they love or hate me. As I said before, blogging is not a one-way form of communication. The comment form allows visitors to voice their opinions and respond to your posts. Someone may come across your blog for the first time and find a particularly interesting article. After reading through it, they may feel inspired to leave a comment. This is great, but many of these visitors may never come back. You need to remind them to come back!

The handy "Subscribe to Comments" WordPress plug-in adds in a small check box next to where readers are able to leave comments. The check box gives readers the opportunity to receive notifications of future comments on that same post. More specifically, the check box reads "Notify me of follow-up comments via e-mail." Seeing how they already provide an e-mail address as part of the comment form, this extra check box already has the information it needs. When a new comment is made to the post, an e-mail is automatically dispatched to the subscriber. This way, readers may feel motivated to come back and respond to the new comment. The more times a person comes back to your blog, the greater likelihood you have of gaining a loyal reader! Better still, each time they come back, they are once again exposed to your RSS feed icon (which is prominently featured, of course) as well as any advertising you may have. More traffic is always a good thing.

Different people have different opinions on the matter, so it's up to you whether or not you want the check box to be ticked by default. Some people say that having the box ticked by default will ensure that all commentators are automatically notified of new comments on your blog, but some of them may view this as spam and, as such, may get a bitter taste in their mouths when it comes to your blog. Other people say that you should not have the box checked by default because if people want to subscribe they can check it themselves. Feel free to run an experiment using both methods so that you can discover for yourself which works better. Your traffic numbers will tell you.

Show Top Commentators

You want to encourage people to comment on your blog. The increased level of activity will attract the attention of new visitors because they'll see a very active community. They'll follow the crowd, and if they see that the crowd likes reading (and commenting on) your blog, they'll be more inclined to do so too. So, how can you encourage people to comment on your blog? By rewarding those who comment the most, of course!

The Show Top Commentators WordPress plug-in encourages feedback and discussion because it rewards people who comment. The plug-in creates a list of people who have left the most comments within a set period of time. Most blogs choose to have the count reset on a monthly basis, but you can also have it reset every week, every year, or you can do what I do and generate a list of people who have left the most comments in the last seven days. You can then post this list on your blog, either in the sidebar or in the footer.

The key motivation, you see, is that the links associated with their names under the Top Commentators system are actually full links with complete "dofollow" link juice. As your blog gets bigger, people will be increasingly more motivated to stay on this list, because it means that they are getting a "live link" back to their own sites. Contrast this to the links in the regular comment area, which typically have the "nofollow" tag. Ever since installing the plug-in, I have seen a drastic increase in the number of comments left on my blog.

Related Posts

Related to what I said in chapter 4 about the importance of deeplinking to your posts, the RelatedPosts plug-in adds in a list of related posts to the end of every article you publish on your blog. It does this on a rather rudimentary level, largely based on the keywords you used in the current post, but it does so in a reasonably effective manner. The previously published material can then receive new life from visitors who may not have read it before. You can try prefacing the list with something like "If you liked this post, you might also like these" or something along those lines. Linking to related posts is a great way to generate extra page views and keep readers on your blog. I recommend that you install the code on the individual post pages only, though, and not on the main index page. Otherwise, your main index page will start to look really cluttered.

RunPHP and Digg This

It's important to take advantage of several traffic generation methods. By and large, blog owners only look at two things: search engine optimization and the increasing the number of RSS subscribers. These two avenues will generate a large portion of your site's traffic, but you can also gain a lot of traffic through social bookmarking sites. Digg. com is probably one of the most popular real-time bookmarking sites, particularly for people interested in technology and the Web. It was through a series of consecutive front-page Diggs that John Chow Dot Com got its first real break. As I described in an earlier chapter, the Diggs served as the ramp for my blog.

Getting yourself noticed on Digg can be one of the important accomplishments of your early blogging career. In order to better promote a particularly good article on Digg, you might want to take advantage of your preexisting readers. To do this, you'll need to install two very valuable WordPress plug-ins.

The first is DiggThis, a WordPress plug-in that detects incoming links from Digg.com and automatically displays a link back to the Digg post. This way, site visitors can go to Digg.com and Digg your story. The more Diggs you can get within a short amount of time, the more likely you'll get bumped onto the front page and experience what is called the "Digg effect." This occurs when you receive a massive influx of traffic; many shared web-hosting plans have trouble dealing with this level of traffic. Thankfully, I have a dedicated web host for my blog, and as your blog gets up to that level of popularity, you may want to invest in dedicated web hosting as well. Getting back to the DiggThis plug-in, it will recognize an incoming Digg and send an e-mail to let you know that someone has Dugg your story. There are many options to choose from and a variety of ways to display the incoming Digg. The most popular way is a button that displays the current number of Diggs a story has received. This is updated in nearly real time!

The second plug-in that you'll need is called RunPHP. As its name implies, it allows you to execute PHP code inside a blog post. Normally, this is not possible. The main reason I run this plug-in is because it allows me to choose which blog posts display the DiggThis button. Without RunPHP, I would be displaying the DiggThis button at the top of every post, and this would be seriously depressing, because most posts don't get Dugg. You do not want to show a Digg Count of zero. By using RunPHP, you can install the DiggThis button code after the story has already been Dugg.

Total WordPress Backup

Always backup your work! The last thing you want to happen is to find that your web host has crashed, or that someone has hacked into your blog, causing you to lose all the hard work that you have put into it. Doing a complete backup of your blog consists of two very simple steps, and you should be doing this on a fairly regular basis. I've heard far too many horror stories about a site getting hacked and the blogger not having an up-to-date backup of his materials.

The first step is to install a WordPress plug-in called, appropriately enough, WordPress Database Backup. This plug-in performs a complete backup of your entire WordPress database, which contains all the content of your blog, including every blog post, every comment, your category structure, and all those other integral elements. Without the database, your site is just an empty shell. After installing and activating the plug-in, go to the Manage tab in your WordPress control panel, and click on "Backup." From there you'll be able to choose a number of different ways to backup your WordPress database. You can download the backup file directly, or you can have it e-mailed to the address of your choice. For an automated solution, the system can automatically send an updated database backup to your e-mail address at regular intervals. That said, I choose to turn the plug-in off after I have backed up my database, for security reasons.

The second step is to back up the uploads, plug-ins, and layout information for your blog. The database contains the actual content (words), while another part of your site stores how this material is presented. The easiest way to back up all the images you have uploaded to the server, as well as all the information related to your custom WordPress theme, is to go into your favorite FTP program and save the entire wp-content folder. As your blog gets bigger and older, this part of the backup can take a fair bit longer. To circumvent this, you can opt for mirroring services and other redundancy-saving methods through your web host.

Contact Form

Sometimes your readers will want to contact you directly. Potential advertisers may also want to reach you directly. It's crucial that you open up these lines of communication because a question posted in the comments section of your blog could easily be overlooked. Moreover, some of this information could be on the private side of things — like inquiring about private advertising or placing a paid review on your blog—so you should offer a quick and easy way for people to e-mail you.

As you know, it may not necessarily be in your best interest to publicly display your e-mail address. This can open you up to all sorts of hacking, spamming, and other bad things. To circumvent this issue while making yourself just as available to your readers, you can use a great WordPress plug-in, the WPContact Form. This plug-in creates a set of code that produces a simple contact form, giving space for the visitor to supply his name, e-mail address, and a personal message. To help reduce the amount of spam, you can also include one of those anti-spam questions in the form. Use a simple arithmetic question; those usually work best.

The contact form code can then quickly and easily be converted into a single page on your blog. Users simply click on that, just as they would to access your About page or Advertising page, to send you a quick e-mail. In the future, I hope that a simple "service ticket" system is developed for WordPress (so that the "conversation" can be tracked, just like when you send in a product for warranty service), but the contact form works almost as well.

Chapter Seven:
Content is King

In this chapter, we'll discuss the importance of quality content and how you can go about providing it.

There is something on your blog that is much more important than any search engine optimization or advertising technique. It's more important than what marketing strategies you employ, or how you design your blog. By far, the most important aspect of your blog is the actual content. Without great content, no one is going to visit your blog in the first place. And those that do happen to stumble across your place on the Internet? Well, they're probably never going to come back. It might sound a little clichéd, but having quality content will always be the number one driver of traffic to your blog. Content is king.

People come to John Chow Dot Com because they're interested in the material I present. They might find the articles I write to be informative, entertaining, or a little of both. Whatever the case, it gets people to come back to my blog each and every day, and this is what you should be trying to do with your blog as well. This is why you should never fall victim to a situation where you feel compelled to post something just because you feel like you should be posting something. No one likes filler content, and your readers will see right through it. At the same time, you might want to lighten the mood every so often with a funny video you found on YouTube. The exact strategy for posting what is considered "quality content" will vary from niche to niche, blog to blog. You'll have to find the formula that works best for you.

What is Quality Content?

Contrary to popular belief, there is no precise definition of "quality content." For some people, true quality content is a truly groundbreaking post. I don't think this is true. Quality content can take on a variety of forms, and the true mark of whether the article is worthwhile can be gauged by both how much attention it receives and how much traffic it generates. You can see the interest in the article by checking out the page views, reading the comments, and finding out how many other blogs have linked to it. Content is the foundation of traffic. Everything starts with content, because without content, you really don't have a blog. By extension, if you don't have quality content, you don't have a quality blog.

By and large, I write most of the content on John Chow Dot Com myself. Even when I allow guest posts from other bloggers, I screen the content heavily to ensure that only the best guest articles make it through and that they're in line with the look and feel of the rest of my articles. If you're going to run a blog, then you should do most of the writing. This can change as your blog grows and matures to more commercial levels—like Engadget and CrunchGear, for example— but when you start out, the content should be mostly yours. Nothing says MFA (Made For AdSense) quite like a blog with free articles all over it. Posts taken from free article services are typically of poor quality, and they'll also be published on a number of other websites. Don't forget that the most unique thing about your blog is *you.* Moreover, you could run into all sorts of duplicate content issues with Google if you make use of free article services.

Your content needs to be good, and it needs to be unique. Write about issues that other people are not writing about, and even when you do write about a concept or idea that has already been discussed, add a new spin to it. You need to infuse your own views and personality into each and every post. The biggest reason why my blog got so big so fast was its content. Why else would someone read a blog? They're interested in what I have to say because it's not the same as what other people may be saying. You will never get very big if all you do is repost the local news. Anyone can regurgitate what has already been said. The truly successful blogger is original. Good content will get you readers and links from other blogs. Good content will get you on the front page of Digg, attention on other social news media sites, and it might even earn you a little fame along the way.

When trying to write truly remarkable content, it's important that your first focus be on exactly that: producing good content. *Don't worry so much about making money from the post. The money will come if your content is good and it is marketed correctly.* Content is the foundation on which your blog is built. Too many people try to put the cart before the horse. They want to see the money, but they don't see the level of work it takes to get there. Producing unique, quality content on a daily basis is not an easy feat to accomplish, which is why you need a topic that you are really passionate about. (Remember that from chapter three?) If you're not actually interested in your niche, then you will have a very difficult time producing the level of content that your blog needs to be successful.

Following the same line of thought, try not to get caught up in the search engine optimization (SEO) end of things either. I took a class in Internet Marketing and SEO, and the teacher kept talking about stuff like key phrases, keyword density, making sure your content is Google-friendly, and so on. As I said before, you should write for people, not for Google. You can have an article that has been optimized for Google in every possible way, but it will still not rank first for your target keyword because Google follows people. When you write quality content, people will read it. When you write with only SEO in mind, the only reader you'll have is Google's spider. Yes, I do keep an eye on my keywords and key phrases when I'm writing a post, but I keep a much closer eye on ensuring that the readers come first. Google comes in at a distant second.

Quality content is something that will be of interest to your readers. Those are the posts that are going to be the most appreciated. Don't get self-indulgent with your blog because while it may be fun to write about your day, is that really what your readers want to see? (Ironically, writing about their boring days works for some bloggers, particularly celebrity bloggers, so go figure.)

Staying Within Your Niche

This is a point of contention among some bloggers. By and large, Web surfers are looking for specific websites to suit their specific needs, and the hunt for the right blogs to read is no exception. I've said countless times that you should blog with passion. It's important that you define your passion —your niche—because that is really the only way that you are going to take your blog to the top.

You've probably heard the saying "Jack-of-all-trades and master of none." This certainly applies to blogging as well. If your blog post ideas are all over the map and there doesn't appear to be any sort of cohesion or connection between your articles, readers will not know what to expect from you, and they may ultimately abandon your blog as a result. It's fine to deviate from your niche from time to time, but it's important that you largely stay focused on what your blog's main topic. Someone coming to a blog about how to raise a puppy will be thrown into a tailspin if all the posts in the last week are about fast cars, hot women, and a new advertising network. In keeping your options open, you're not really catering to any specific audience. Supplement your blog with other quality content, but keep the focus of your blog in mind too.

Perhaps one of the best ways to think about this is to consider the most prestigious restaurants in your area. The best restaurants are always those that decide on a small handful of menu items and prepare them extremely well. People go to a great steak restaurant, believe it or not, to eat steak. They don't go there to try the pasta or the sushi. In contrast, restaurants that try to be all things to all people, offering a wide-ranging menu with a whole bunch of mediocre dishes, ultimately fail. This lack of focus means that no single item on your menu is getting the attention it deserves, and nothing will ever stand out as the superstar. Even if all the dishes at this jack-of-all-trades restaurant are good, the place will never become particularly well-known for anything. *You want your blog to be known for something.* John Chow Dot Com is known for making money online.

Highly Focused Articles Are Best

Don't you hate it when you open up a magazine, start reading an article, and then discover that the author is jumping all over the place, with no sense of cohesion or theme? Then it should come as no surprise that blog readers have the exact same reaction to posts that jump all over the place. The best articles that you can write are those that stay highly focused and address a single issue. When you decide on a blog topic, it should be highly defined. Think about it as a thesis for a college essay or something along those lines. The more focused the topic (or thesis), the better the result because your blog can address this single issue in a very comprehensive and in-depth way.

Vague blog post ideas are no good. They're the ones that end up fluttering about in no man's land without ever coming to a real conclusion. For this reason, when you think of an idea for your next article, ask yourself if it is specific enough. If it's not, there's a good chance that you can spin that original article idea into multiple articles! Don't try to cram too many different ideas into a single post because it will either sound terribly disorganized, or it will result in information overload for your readers.

Finding Blog Post Ideas

I've made hundreds and hundreds of posts since I started John Chow Dot Com in December 2005. Many people have asked how I manage to keep up this level of content generation, especially since I ensure that each and every post provides value to the reader. This value could be in the form of highlighting a new advertising network, or it could just be a goofy video I made at dinner. In either case, visitors have found something useful or entertaining in my posts, and they will continue to come back looking for more quality content. Keeping up this level of content generation really isn't that hard. For my posts, I tend to look at three sources.

In My Head

This might come out sounding a little arrogant, but a lot of my blog post ideas *are my ideas*. These ideas can just come at me at the most random of times, so I make sure to make a note of the idea if I'm not at my computer at the time. For example, I carry my cell phone with me everywhere I go. It doesn't take much effort to whip out the mobile phone and enter a fake entry into the phonebook, record a quick voice memo, or even send myself a voicemail. This is much more convenient that carrying around a pad and paper. Regardless of how you do it, it's important that you write them all down somehow.

It is possible to keep an ongoing flow of quality content if you just keep track of your ideas in an organized manner. Even within the WordPress control panel you can keep a large supply of "drafts," which are basically uncompleted blog posts. If it's a relatively simple idea, then you can just save a draft with little more than a placeholder for the title. If it's a more complex concept that you want to blog about, then it might be worthwhile to include a few notes. You create drafts by using the "Write" tool, just as you normally do to write posts. Now, instead of hitting the "Publish" button, all you do is hit the "Save" button instead. The next time you access the "Write" tool, WordPress will remind you that you have something saved in Drafts. To get a full list of your Drafts, go to the Manage tab, and then select to only view posts that have Draft status.

Ultimately, the most unique thing about your blog is you. If your ideas are good and you express them in an easy to understand manner, people will read your blog. This is partly why John Chow Dot Com has become as popular as it has. People seem to like my (sometimes evil) ideas.

Blog Comments

Even though several of my blog post ideas are self-generated, a lot more of my content ideas come from comments that readers leave on my blog. It's important that you acknowledge the participation and feedback provided by your readers, because these are the people taking valuable time out of their days to visit your blog. If you address their needs in the best possible way, providing them with quality content, they will certainly come back. When I read through the comments left on my blog, I will often find a question or a request from one of the readers. If I feel it's worthwhile, I can answer the question through a full blog post, rather than simply responding with a couple of sentences in the comments section.

This is the best way to produce content because you already know that this is the content your readers are looking for. After all, they asked you for this content directly! You can't get better targeting than giving the readers exactly what they asked for. Chances are, if you do it correctly, the resulting article will lead to future articles, because subsequent readers will have follow-up questions and requests that they will leave in the comments section for that article. It's an ongoing cycle and it will help you to produce some of the best and most relevant content for your readers. This will attract even more readers, even more comments, and—as a result—even more great content. Blogs grow as they address the needs of their readers in better and more comprehensive ways.

But I don't have a lot of readers yet!

It's perfectly understandable that when you're first starting out, you probably don't have a lot of readers. As a result, you also don't have a lot of comments. How, then, can you turn to blog comments for ideas? Simple. Just look at other similar blogs in your niche.

Surfing for Content

When I wake up in the afternoon, I usually don't have any real idea of what I'm going to write about. The first thing I do is read through the blog comments because this is the best source for article ideas. If there is nothing there that piques my interest, I start to surf through the list of websites in my bookmarks. This is my second biggest source of article ideas. I can also look for article ideas from magazines, newspapers, television, the radio, and all sorts of other places. You just have to find something that inspires or interests you, and then you can put your unique spin on the story for your own readers.

When surfing through the Web, I'm really looking for stories that I think would interest my readers. The objective is not to just repost the stories. You're not CNN, so you really shouldn't regurgitate what can be found elsewhere. That would be far too easy. What I want to do is put my own spin on a story, thus adding value to the content and producing something that is actually original. You can also add value by talking about the story and then supplementing it with related information that readers may find useful. You may find a story about an online service that made $50 million last year; you can then add value by offering a clear explanation as to how this service made that amount of money and what they plan on doing in the future to continue to generate that level of revenue. Blogging is all about offering your personal touch. You don't want to report without emotion or opinions because bloggers are expected to get down and dirty with their articles. Make the content your own. Don't be afraid to state your views or piss people off.

But don't just stop at the other articles on the Web! It can also be worthwhile to read the blog comments left on other blogs in your niche because these readers can easily become your readers as well. If you like to blog about professional hockey, for example, it's within reason to think that someone commenting on a related hockey blog would be interested in yours as well. If this person left a question or request on this other hockey blog, there's nothing stopping you from answering that question or fulfilling that request on your own blog. Better still, after you've written your own blog post, you can send a trackback (a message that notifies the original blog of the citation and backlink). Most blogs openly display incoming trackbacks, so you can gain attention from readers who will probably be interested in your quality content, assuming your content is of good quality to begin with, of course.

Where Else to Get Quality Content

What do you do if you can't write content yourself? The best and hardest way to create content is writing it yourself, but it can be the most time-consuming too. If you really know the topic that you're covering, then you should be the one writing for your blog. After all, what's your blog if you're not in it? Even so, it can valuable to supplement your quality content with some great writing from a few other sources. Here are a few areas that I have explored on my own blog; consider checking them out.

Hire Someone to Write

This will depend somewhat on the nature of your blog, but if you have a great idea for an article, it's perfectly feasible to hire someone else to write it for you. This is a particularly good strategy if you are tapping into their particular area of expertise, especially if they know more about the topic than you do. For example, if you have a blog that largely talks about computer games and then you come up with a great post idea that talks a little more about console games instead, it might be a better idea to get a console game guy to write the post, because he's probably more knowledgeable when it comes to console games (assuming that you're a PC gamer). Even if you have equal knowledge with the other writer, having extra people around to produce content can only help the growth of your blog. As I have said several times before, without content, your blog is nothing. The more *quality* content you have on your site, the more likely you'll be able to attract a larger audience.

Many tech sites, for example, employ a stable of writers, each of whom may specialize in a certain area. There will be one person who's really good with multimedia gadgets, whereas another person is better equipped to write about internal computer components. This takes advantage of their individual areas of expertise. You are still focusing on a certain niche, but you are exploring different areas within that niche so that you can attract as many readers as possible. This will help you to increase your traffic. The added bonus is that these writers will be motivated to promote their own content too; they'll have no problem telling their friends about a great article they wrote *on your blog*. Guess what? That's more traffic for you.

How you choose to pay these writers is up to you. There are several different ways that you can handle payment. If your blog is big and commercial—like those in Gawker Media—then it might not be a bad idea to have full-time writers on salary. Many other blogs choose to pay on a per-word or per-article basis. Alternatively, you can choose to offer some sort of performance-based payment system wherein the writer gets more money if his or her article gets a certain number of page views. It's even possible to get writers to write for free! Many tech sites don't pay anything, but instead allow their writers to keep the review items after they've completed the review. Whatever method you choose, it's in your best interest to have some sort of contract outlining how payment works and who owns the content (you). The last thing you want is to find these articles posted on other sites too.

When I get a paid review request on John Chow Dot Com, a considerable source of income for my blog, I will often hand the task off to Michael Kwan to complete. Most people who pay for a review on my blog are not necessarily looking for a review from me; instead, they're much more interested in the exposure that they'll receive from being featured on my blog. By getting Michael Kwan to do the actual review, I can spend more time focusing on creating original quality content of my own, and that's where John Chow Dot Com gets its truly original and unique content: from John Chow.

Ask Readers to Guest Blog

While you may have a pretty good idea about what your blog readers want to read, the readers themselves can provide some fantastic content as well. Better still, they can be in good touch with what your readers want because they *are* readers. The trouble with asking for guest articles from your reader is that most of the submissions are not usable. Everyone seems to want their fifteen minutes of fame and having their article published on their favorite site (yours) is one way to go about it. Unfortunately, many of these readers are good *readers*, but they're not very good *writers*. The article quality can be quite poor and you don't want to associate these blog posts with your brand and your blog.

You should be very selective about the guest posts you publish on your blog because even though the byline belongs to someone else, the content is still associated with you. Also, be sure to make it clear to guest bloggers that all submitted content becomes your property, and that they cannot republish the article anywhere else, both online and offline. As your blog gets bigger, there will be more people who will be interested in getting their articles published on your blog. I know this is true with John Chow Dot Com. I only publish work from bloggers who I respect and who I would enjoy reading myself.

In exchange for providing free content for your blog, most readers will want a backlink to their own blog as well. This is only fair, and I usually allow them to have a one-sentence write-up either at the beginning or the end of the post that describes who they are, what they do, and where readers can find out more. If I were to do a guest blog post for someone else, I'd only expect the same in kind.

Trade Articles with Other Sites

Using this strategy is similar to the one described above, except you are offering something in exchange with another blog in your niche. You don't have to think about these other sites as competition. It's actually very important to network with other sites in your niche! When you trade articles with other blogs, you don't necessarily have to write a completely new post for them, just as they don't have to write a completely new post for you. One of the most effective strategies for getting new quality content for both your blogs is simply to dig into the archives.

But won't I run into the duplication penalty from Google?

No! I'm not saying that you should simply fish out an old article that you wrote for your blog and ship it off to the other blog to use. What you should do is take an older post and then rewrite enough of it so that it will avoid the duplication penalty. You don't have to come up with any new ideas or concepts, because you've already addressed these in the existing post. If the content is a little out of date, then just update the post with more current information. Rework the structure a little, choose some new words, and that will be enough for it to be original again.

The big advantage to this strategy is that to the readers of the other person's blog, your old article is new stuff. The same is true of the refreshed article that the other blogger exchanged for yours. Both sets of readers are presented with something that they haven't seen before and everyone is happy. It's a win-win situation.

Republish Old Posts

What do you get when you take the previously described strategy and then employ it with your own websites? If you happen to own several related blogs, it's perfectly possible for to be on both ends of the equation, swapping old articles across your other blogs. The same guidelines apply as before, because you'll likely want to pull an older article and then do a bit of rewriting so that it brings the article up-to-date, and it varies the content enough that you won't run into a duplication penalty from Google and other search engines.

I have used this strategy to cross-post content on not only the TechZone, but also on Laptop Gamer and Digital Grabber. Depending on the context, I have also tried doing this with articles originally posted on John Chow Dot Com, giving the article a bit more of a highlight on the TechZone. In fact, I've had an article or two get picked up on the TechZone that may not otherwise have generated the same level of attention on John Chow Dot Com. You'll want to do some rewriting, but maximizing your value from minimal effort can work wonders in your favor.

Where You Shouldn't Go to Get Content

In an effort to continually generate quality content for your readers, you may be tempted to take on alternative strategies in ensuring that there is a new post each and every day. Unfortunately, many of these shortcuts can only harm you in the long run. Here are three ways to get content that I highly recommend you avoid. You might even be better off occasionally *not* posting new content instead of using one of these techniques on a continual basis. They may sound appealing, but they are ultimately harmful.

Scraping from RSS Feeds

The one distinctive feature that you will find on most Made for AdSense (MFA) websites is an abundance of uncategorized content. That's because these websites don't produce any content of their own; instead, they steal articles from other websites through RSS feeds. This practice is known as scraping. These are the Google whores that take the easy way out. All they do is pull in a bunch of feeds from a number of sites, and then they republish the material on their own sites. Most of these people are also pretty lazy, so they keep all the backlinks intact. The content might be decent, but this is no different than stealing, and it's not something that you want to associate yourself with.

You may have even come across some get-rich-quick schemes that are designed around this practice. They will sell you an entire system based on RSS feeds wherein you are able to enter different categories, like technology or health, and it will generate "free" content for you by stealing the feeds of content that fits these categories . A site is generated and the ad revenue is supposed to just start rolling in. As you can imagine, this strategy is not very effective. This isn't to say that using RSS feeds to add to your site content is a completely bad idea, but the RSS feeds should not serve as your site's main content. Use other feeds as inspiration, and you can even get away with using excerpts as occasional filler.

Private Label Articles

Private label rights (PLR) can be defined as an intellectual property right that allows you to modify a work—like an article—and claim the work as your own. The caveat is that the actual copyright is granted to neither the original work nor the modified work. Private label articles can give users a really quick way to get a lot of content up on their sites, and the price for these rights is remarkably low as well. It's pretty easy to get yourself up to two hundred private label articles for as little as fifteen cents each. This means that two hundred articles will cost you a measly thirty bucks. Because you are legally allowed to edit these works as you see fit and then attach your name to the piece as if it were your own, PLR articles can be a great source of ideas.

Why don't more bloggers make use of PLR articles? Honestly, most of the articles available through PLR are pieces of junk. They're poorly written and the ideas aren't the best. After going through and rewriting the article so heavily, it's not really worth it to pay for private label rights. You're better off just creating the original content yourself. This way, you get to keep the copyright as well.

The other major issue with PLR articles is duplication and replication. As you can imagine, you won't be the only one who will be using any given private label article. This will seriously hurt your search engine rankings and some of your readers might notice that the article was published elsewhere. This can create a lot of confusion because people will see the same article published in a number of places and by many different authors. The content gets severely diluted in this way. PLR articles just aren't worth it, even if they are only fifteen cents a piece. That's fifteen cents you can spend somewhere else.

Free Article Services

If you thought that PLR articles were junk, then you should really avoid free article services like the plague. Think about it. If an article that costs fifteen cents is a piece of garbage, how good do you think the free article really is? Even so, free article services have become the favorite playground for many Google whores and other people who are looking to get rich quick. The articles are free and nearly limitless. Too bad they are, well, really bad. And as with the PLR articles, you are going to run into all sorts of content duplication problems; it's just not worth the headache.

In the end, it's unique content that's going to drive traffic to your site and the best source for unique content is, you guessed it, *you*! It can be tempting to take advantage of free article services even as filler, but the best strategy is to avoid them if at all possible.

Would You Read This?

In your quest to provide quality content that is actually useful, informative, or even entertaining, it can sometimes be difficult to discern if you're doing the right thing. When you write an article, it's a good idea to stop and think for a moment. Would you read this? Would you find value in this article if you were to find it on another blog? Asking these kinds of questions could prove to be one of the best tests to determine whether your blog is worth reading or not. I talk a lot about how content is king and how you need to have unique quality content for your blog to rise to the top. Be honest with yourself. If you don't really want to read it, if you don't really want to subscribe to your own blog, why would anyone else want to?

Chapter Eight:
Promotion and
Search Engine Optimization

In this chapter, we'll explore the different promotional techniques that you can employ, in addition to several methods of optimizing your blog for search engines.

So you've decided on your niche and you're creating some truly original content. This is some of the best writing you've done in your life, and you're quite proud of what's been said so far on your blog. The trouble is, no one is reading it. Contrary to *Field of Dreams* wisdom, if you build it, they might not come. You have to tell them to come. You have to invite them to come. Getting noticed on the Internet, especially when there are well over one hundred million blogs out there (and growing), is quite the challenging task. Creating quality content is just one part of the equation. Another very important part is promotion. Business types might refer to it as marketing, but they're really the same thing.

How can you get the rest of the Web to notice your blog? Well, you'll find that the major backbone to getting noticed is getting backlinks. The more links that point to your blog (and specific blog posts), the better chance you have of being noticed. You'll still need quality content to entice these new visitors to stick around, but if you manage to build up some links on a few bigger sites, this can work wonders for your traffic figures. It helps if you already have a little bit of traffic and some loyal subscribers because they can help you spread the word about some of your better posts.

I wrote a post a long while back called "The Internet's Biggest Google Whores" and it listed the top eight Google AdSense income earners at the time. It got boatloads of attention because it had a good title and the content was interesting to anyone looking to make money online. One of my readers Dugg it, and it quickly reached Digg's front page. I got links from thousands of sites, and to this day, I still get new sites linking to that article. This goes to show you that quality content really works, but you need a promotional tool to get it over that hump. Digg served as the catapult for that particular article.

Six Favorite Linking Strategies

Getting backlinks is more of an art than it is a science, but there are a few strategies that have worked quite well for me in the past. These links can act as great promotional tools because they expose your blog to an ever-expanding audience. Each blog that links to you has a specific readership, and if someone in there picks up the story, you've got another set of readers; the process can go on and on.

1. Visit Other Blogs on a Regular Basis

Get to know the other bloggers in your niche and develop these relationships without the intention of immediately benefiting from them. When you are friends with other bloggers, they are more likely to link to you anyway, so you don't even need to ask them (though asking doesn't hurt if done in moderation). It was because of the TechZone that I got to meet so many other like-minded individuals. In a similar manner, my work on John Chow Dot Com—and my subsequent visits to other related blogs—helped me to get in touch with other professional bloggers. As you can imagine, there's a lot to be gained here beyond just backlinks! Learn from one another and you can mutually benefit.

Don't simply visit other blogs in your niche on a regular basis; leave comments on their posts and use their contact forms to introduce yourself. This is usually enough to get blog owners to notice you, and they might pay your blog a visit. If you have great content on your blog, there's a good chance that they will become a regular reader, possibly subscribing to your RSS feed. As they encounter more of your quality posts, there's a good chance that they'll start linking to your posts on their own blog.

This is also why it's helpful to get involved with blogging communities like BlogCatalog and MyBlogLog. Many bloggers take a look at their community pages quite often to see who has joined. They might pay a visit to the blogs of the new members and, again, if the quality content is there, a new backlink may be delivered. It's all about getting your name out there; if they know you, they'll visit. It's only when they visit that you'll have a chance of getting linked.

2. Get Backlinks By Giving Them Out

Give and you shall receive. It pays to be generous in the blogosphere, and backlinks serve as currency. When you link to another blog, several things happen. First, the other blog will typically get notified via a trackback or a pingback. This shows up in their WordPress dashboard, and many bloggers are just plain interested in what other sites are saying about them; we're all a little egocentric. Although we may or may not change our habits as a result, we all want to know what other people are thinking about us, and blogging is no exception. When you get a link from another blog, there's a good chance that you'll want to check them out, right?

Bam! You just got yourself a visitor.

If you have good content (see how it always comes back to having quality content?), then there's a chance that you'll get a linkback in the process. When you link to others without asking for anything in return, you'll likely grab the attention of at least a couple of the recipients. When I dole out link love to the blogging community, I sometimes find that some of the recipients will make a new blog post proudly exclaiming that they got a link from John Chow! It's flattering, to be sure, but the exact same strategy can work for you as well. Link to other blogs, and you'll probably get some links in return.

3. The Targeted News Release

This strategy probably isn't as effective for personal blogs, but if you have timely blog posts about something, particularly if you've put together a valuable resource, reviewed something interesting, or highlighted a new product or service in the marketplace, a news release just might work. It's certainly helpful to build a news list of blogs that cover the same niche as you do because they can be your best source for backlinks! When you have an interesting article, you can send out a news release to your fellow bloggers telling them about it. The news release doesn't have to be too long either; it just has to have enough that the recipients will want to read further. If your article is good, most blogs will link to you.

News releases represent one of the biggest sources of traffic and backlinks for the TechZone. We maintain a list of over 1,000 technology news sites and when we have new content, I send out a news release to all of these sites. You probably shouldn't go to the well too often—the other sites might get annoyed and start to think of you as spam, rather than as an informative blog—but news releases can be very effective. Welcome to traffic and link heaven.

4. Try Some Linkbaiting

Quality content is the path that you want to take most of the time because it is the path that will result in the most loyal readers. These are the readers that you want to work your hardest to keep. Even so, when you're first starting out you just want all the attention you can get. For times like those, consider the art of linkbaiting and creating viral content. Believe it or not, these can result in some great quality content as well.

Linkbait is anything interesting enough to catch people's attention (and anything interesting enough to, well, bait links). On one level, it's something that's designed to get the attention of anyone and everyone who reads it. On another level, it can be highly targeted attention-getting. I have been the target of several linkbaiting ideas, like when people have decided to feature a comical version of me in a music video with other top bloggers. These kinds of videos do a good job of getting my attention, so long as they are done well and in an entertaining way. Producing content with the main purpose of grabbing people's attention isn't necessarily a bad thing; you just have to be creative. And this is also how content can get viral. Think about some of the most popular videos on YouTube! They may not be the most useful or informative, but they sure get a lot of views.

If you're willing to put in the work, some of the best linkbaits are the articles that go at length to report on something. They'll compile a large amount of data that other people couldn't be bothered to collect, and then they present their findings in an easy-to-understand manner. In the past, people have compared the effectiveness of e-mail spam filters, for example, on various free online e-mail domains. Most people couldn't be bothered to sift through their spam folders on a continual basis, let alone record all the false negatives and false positives! This is a lot of work, but it *can* be rewarding.

Another strategy for linkbaiting is to say something controversial because this will surely generate discussion if you do it correctly. This method gets old really fast if you use it too much, and you risk alienating some of your readers for being controversial on purpose. It'll show. If you truly feel a certain way, then don't be afraid to express your opinion; that's one thing. It's another thing altogether to try and piss people off on purpose.

To be truly successful at the art of linkbaiting, you have to look at linking as a fishing expedition. You need to dangle some enticing bait out there, and then you wait until the fish "bite." In the context of developing a successful blog, the bait is your content, and the fish are the other websites on the Internet. A somewhat evil and deceptive way to dangle bait is to ask for a review on a webmaster forum. This is very effective when your blog is still new, because it looks like a genuine request (and it kind of is). When you ask the members of the forum to review your site and provide feedback, you're effectively getting them to visit your site and take a nice, long look around. As the recommendations start to come in, you can then make some adjustments to your blog. Then you ask the forum, "How about now?" Guess what? You just got another wave of visitors!

Other linkbaiting strategies you can try include writing about the site you wish to bait—there are so many people writing about John Chow Dot Com these days—or interviewing a site owner. If done correctly, that site owner will then mention the interview on his or her own site. After all, they like having their egos stroked too, just like everyone else. Another strategy: if you happen to attend a trade show, try to get a popular blogger to pose with a booth babe. Post this picture on your blog, and then tell the popular blogger about it. He will no doubt link to that story!

5. Submit Articles to Social Networking Sites

You may have noticed that social networking sites and social bookmarking sites have quickly risen in popularity the past few years. You could say that it's due to the whole Web 2.0 phenomenon wherein Internet content is more user-driven than ever. People don't want to just passively ingest the things that they encounter on the Web; they want to interact with it. In this way, you can take advantage of these kinds of websites by submitting your articles to them. There are applications in Facebook, for example, that automatically fetch your RSS feed and post a note in your profile, telling your friends that you have put up a new article on your blog. There is also an application called Blog Friends where users insert a box in their profile that highlights posts from their blogger friends. If you have several friends on this service, then you'll get more exposure when their Facebook friends view your posts.

It's also incredibly useful to utilize social bookmarking sites and social news sites because many Web surfers use these services to find the latest, greatest, and hottest topics on the Internet today. There are many of these social bookmarking sites, so try your hand at a few to see which are the most successful for you. Some examples include del.icio.us, Furl, Reddit, and StumbleUpon. Speaking for myself, both in terms of John Chow Dot Com and the TechZone, I have probably had the most success with Digg.com. In fact, several of my articles have been bumped onto the front page of Digg, resulting in overflowing floods of visitors. Moreover, many bloggers like to link to stories that are showcased on Digg, so getting on the front page can result in a flood of backlinks as well. As I said, lots of links can result in lots of traffic. This improves your search engine performance too.

Again, you have to have compelling and interesting content for sites like Digg and StumbleUpon to pick it up. I've found that Digg users really like lists, and they really like posts that talk about Digg users. My strategy for getting Dugg worked really well for me. I would write an article, have it submitted to Digg, and then try to get as many people to vote for it (Digg it) as possible. The story would then hit the front page, and I'd get tons of traffic and links. Rinse and repeat as needed. It seems that I may have overused this strategy a little, because after thirty-plus front-page Diggs, I was banned. However, it was too late for the haters to stop my rise. Far too many Digg users were already exposed to my blog, and they liked what they saw. Mission accomplished.

6. Blogging Contests: Value to Them, Free to You

Hosting a contest on your blog could be one of the most effective promotional strategies because you get to make the rules. Before you set out on your first blog contest, you should determine the explicit goal or objective of the contest. Is it to increase the number of RSS subscribers? Is it to increase the number of backlinks to your blog from other sites? Is it to help improve the level of discussion on your blog via the comments? Each of these objectives is quite distinct, and you should arrange the rules of your contest around these goals.

For example, if the goal is to increase the volume of comments on your blog—this increased activity level can serve to show new visitors that your blog's a popular website, and one that other people enjoy reading—then you can say that the winner of the contest will be the person who has the most comments within a certain time period. The Top Commentators plug-in is especially useful for this purpose.

Alternatively, if the goal is to increase the number of RSS subscribers, you can see how increasing the number of comments does little to achieve this objective. Instead, you can tell people to subscribe via e-mail and you'll pick a winner at random. You can also use a WordPress plug-in to insert a secret message in the RSS feed and tell people that the first one to spot the secret message will be given a prize. You can tell readers that the message will appear some time in the next month, for instance, and if they want to win they'll have to keep their eyes open for it every day.

But I don't want to spend so much money on prizes…

You don't have to. The beauty of a blogging contest is that it doesn't really have to cost you anything. It's not that hard to get other websites and blogs to *sponsor* your contest, offering the prizes out of their pockets in exchange for exposure on your blog. Alternatively, you can offer something of value to the potential winner, even though it's basically free to you. This could be in the form of a "paid" review on your blog, or another form of "paid" advertising on your blog. To create the greatest value to the winner, you can try bundling a few of these things together for the top prize. Give them a two-month sidebar link, a paid review, and some free swag from another website; that's starting to sound like a rather lucrative prize pack.

How to Promote Your RSS Feed

As a blogger, one of the best indicators of the popularity of your blog is the number of people who subscribe to your blog via RSS. This can arguably be more important than how well you rank in search engines, or what your overall traffic figures may look like because RSS subscribers represent loyal readers of your blog. They are your lifeblood, and for this reason you should do everything in your power to increase the number of subscribers. Yes, an RSS feed is much harder to monetize that direct visits to your blog, but a loyal reader base is much more valuable in the long run.

You do not want to be known as a fly-by-night operation. You want to attract people who will be reading your blog for years to come (assuming that blogs will still be popular years from now). Furthermore, the more subscribers, the more comments you'll likely have on your posts. This level of activity will attract even more readers because they want to be involved with something that everyone else seems to be enjoying.

Another major reason to grow your RSS subscriber base is that many ad networks—like ReviewMe—take RSS subscriptions into account when determining your price. The more RSS subscribers you have, the higher your price will be. This makes sense from an advertiser's standpoint because it represents the number of (nearly) guaranteed people who will be reading the paid review. Getting twenty thousand people to read a review is much more valuable than getting two hundred people.

If you want to grow your RSS numbers, then you'll need to offer a full feed. I mentioned earlier that Feedburner has a useful "chicklet" that displays the number of RSS readers on your blog. This number represents the number of people who accessed the blog via RSS the day before. You should not display this chicklet until the number is a little higher, because if a reader arrives at your blog and sees that only 5 people subscribe, they'll assume that your content is pretty crappy (even if it's not). It's best not to show the chicklet until the number hits at least fifty. Big RSS numbers make people want to subscribe; small numbers make them want to leave.

In chapter five I said that you should ensure that your RSS feed is featured prominently on your blog. The button should be placed near the top of every page, and it should be visible without scrolling. This tells people who use RSS aggregators that you have a feed. I also label the button with "Full Feed RSS" to inform them that the feed contains all the content, rather than just excerpts. In the beginning, you might want to use a bigger button that normal to attract attention. As your site becomes more popular, visitors might start to actively seek out the button, and you won't need to make it quite so big. Even so, it should be clearly visible and easy to see.

Don't be afraid to be a little redundant. Ultimately one of the best ways to promote your RSS feed is to simply ask your readers to subscribe. At the end of every post, add a line that says something like, "If you like this post, then consider subscribing to my full feed RSS." You can edit this right into the single.php (or page.php) file in your WordPress template, instead of typing it out each and every time. It's up to you whether you want to include it on the main index page as well, but it could start to look a little annoying there.

Offline Promotion Methods

Your blog is online, so why should you bother with offline methods? Believe or not, there are real people behind all those blogs you read and those real people actually interact in the real world. Some of the best promotion that I have done is through real world contact. From networking with fellow bloggers to getting some press in traditional newspapers, I take advantage of every opportunity that I get to promote my blog. It's all about getting your name out there because not everyone is quite as savvy as you may believe. Some people don't know what RSS is and some people may not even be all that familiar with blogs in the first place. You need to educate them, and you need to pique their interest. Give them a reason to visit your blog and—here it comes again—if you have quality content, they'll come back. A loyal reader is always the best kind of reader.

So, what kinds of offline promotional methods do I recommend? Let's go through some of my favorites.

Business Cards

Blogging isn't just a hobby of yours, so you should give it the respect that it deserves. Seeing how you intend on making money from your blog, you should treat it like a real business. Think about it. You have to deal with satisfying your customers (readers), you have to deal with marketing (promotion), you have to take a look at expenses (cost of hosting, etc.), and so on. It's a business like any other, so it's definitely a good idea to get some business cards for your blog. They make great promotional tools, and they help to legitimize your blog. People are more likely to take you seriously when you hand them a business card, and it helps to build the branding of your blog. They're really inexpensive too. My local print shop can produce one thousand full-color business cards for as low as $85. That's double-sided too! While you could save money by making business cards at home, this is not a good idea. The cheapness will reflect poorly on you and on your blog. When you're online, people don't get to see your fancy office building with valet parking. Their only point of contact with you, besides your blog, is your business card. Make it stand out.

Use Your Car As A Billboard

When you're driving around town, you're probably doing it in your car. Why not take advantage of that opportunity and use your car as a billboard? It's easy enough to go to your local sign shop and get them to make some vinyl stickers with the name and URL of your blog. You can even take the more affordable route and get generic letters, cutting them out yourself and sticking them on your car. This method doesn't need to be as loud and in-your-face as some of the other branded cars you may see on the road, but having a subtle sticker on your rear window can be a great marketing strategy. It's all about taking every opportunity that you've got to get your name (and the URL of your blog) out there in the public eye. You may be online, but *everyone* is offline.

If you are prepared to take the quantum leap, you can even try wrapping your car in a branded design. This will certainly cost more money, but there are several advantages. The wrap does a good job at protecting the vehicle's paint, so when it comes time to sell the car, just remove the wrap and the paint job will look factory-fresh. The other major advantage is that you are able to write off the cost of the wrap as a business expense. It's much easier justifying to the tax man that you use your car for business when it's a moving billboard. In this way, you can write off portions of things like gas, insurance, and maintenance.

I must say, though, that you might only want to use the vinyl sticker and wrap method if you have a half-decent car. If you're putt-putting around town in an old beater, that might not be the image to associate with your blog. Cool car, cool site. Run-down, piece-of-crap car, guess what? Run-down, piece-of-crap site.

Promotional Pens and Other Items

Everyone likes a free gift, right? When you find yourself at a trade show, a networking event, or any other opportunity to meet people who could help with the promotion of your blog, it's not a bad idea to give them a free pen featuring the name and URL of your blog. This works wonders for real-world businesses, so why not try it with online businesses? Many people may see a business card and then forget about it, possibly throwing it away in the trash shortly afterwards. These exact same people, however, are much more inclined to keep a pen or a T-shirt. Pens are a really effective offline promotion item because they're so inexpensive to produce (less than a dollar each) and they do a great job at reinforcing your brand. The thing with a pen is that people are always using them, so by having the name of your blog in their hands so often, they're bound to remember you.

Don't be afraid to wear shirts with your own blog branding on it. Promotional T-shirts are relatively inexpensive as well. Whether you're walking through the trade show floor, spending a lazy Sunday shopping with the family, you're acting as a walking billboard for your blog. Better still, when you give these shirts away to your readers—try hosting a contest!—they can act as your walking billboards too. They're happy because they got a free T-shirt, and you're happy because you're getting all sorts of real-world exposure. If you do choose to produce T-shirts for your blog, be sure to send one to Jeremy Schoemaker (http://www.shoemoney.com), because he has a weekly feature on his blog called Free Shirt Friday. In those posts, he takes a picture of himself wearing a promotional shirt, accompanied by a short blurb about the shirt's blog or company. You can't get cheaper advertising than that on such a popular blog.

Other promotional products to consider should be based on the niche that your blog is trying to capture. Mouse pads can be pretty popular, as can lanyards, coffee mugs, frisbees, calendars, pen holders, and other desktop items; the list goes on and on. Be creative.

Brand Everything Visible

Maybe you do some of your blogging at the local coffee shop. While everyone else is proudly displaying the logos of Apple, HP, and Dell, you can do the same for your blog! Getting a custom sticker or skin from your local printing shop is a very inexpensive endeavor, but can you imagine how much extra exposure you get by plastering the name and URL of your blog on the lid of your laptop? Set up camp by one of the window seats with the lid of your notebook computer facing the adjacent street. Everyone who passes by that coffee shop will see your brand. When you think about how much other companies pay for billboards and street signage, the price of a custom notebook skin sounds like an exceptional deal.

Don't stop at just the lid of your laptop. For anything that will be seen by a lot of people, think about ways that you can use this exposure to your advantage. I've even seen some people leave their business card or a promotional pen behind at the restrooms of restaurants and shopping malls. Whatever it takes, right?

Take Advantage of Local Networking

International trade shows in your niche are pretty great, but be sure to also take advantage of local networking events. Whatever your niche may be, there's a good chance that there's a group of local people with similar interests and they probably meet on a regular basis. There are local blogger groups for more general gatherings as well. These kinds of events attract a lot of like-minded people and are a perfect target audience. When you do attend local networking events like these, be sure to bring along some business cards and a few promotional pens! This can be your time to shine.

Give a Keynote Speech or a Lecture

Do you want to establish yourself as an expert in your niche? You'd be surprised how easy it is to get your way into giving a speech or lecture. I've received a few offers to do a keynote speech at certain events. When you give a keynote speech, your name will appear on the program, typically along with the name of your company (blog) and the URL. This gives you more exposure to a really targeted audience. They want to hear what you have to say, because they're looking to you as an expert. Keynoting is a great way to give your blog a plug and spread your name to a whole new group of people. Keynoting will usually only come around after you've become well-known, but it can take you from being a small-time celebrity to an established expert in your field. After knocking down one or two keynotes, you'll be invited to speak at many more.

If your niche has more of an educational slant to it, it might be possible for you to give a guest lecture or a speech at a local university or college. This doesn't even need to be part of a class and it could just be a casual lecture given during lunch hour. It can cost a little money to book a lecture hall, but after you've made the effort and put up a few flyers, you might actually get a few listeners. The thing is, it doesn't matter how many people actually attend. After you've completed your lecture, you can proudly say on your blog that you gave a lecture at XYZ University. This gives you a certain level of credibility and can further your expert status.

Fear of public speaking has been ranked as being more common than the fear of death. To get some practice speaking in front of a crowd and to get over those initial jitters, try joining the local chapter of Toastmasters International. You'll learn a lot about giving a speech … and then you'll be a great MC at your best friend's wedding reception! (Don't forget to plug your blog there, too.)

Old World Coverage: Newspapers, Radio, and TV

Do you realize how difficult it is to fill a paper with news? Newspapers are *always* looking for good story ideas, so they might as well write about you. The key is to give them a reason. Why are you special? Why is your blog different or unique?

Getting the local newspaper to write about you is a great way to increase your brand presence and make the locals aware of you. Journalists will be more than glad to entertain your proposal. After all, a great story idea just fell in their lap, and they didn't have to actively look for it. I'm sure you'd agree that a story about a local boy making a big splash on the Internet is better than a story about a cat stuck in a tree, or some old granny who likes collecting buttons. The easiest way to get local press is to send a letter to the newspaper editor. This letter should tell them who you are, what you do, and why your story is worthwhile. It should also mention that you are available for an interview.

I recommend that you start with the biggest paper in town and work your way down. You might not get your first choice or even your second choice, but it's always better to shoot for the stars and come up a little short than to grab the lowest hanging fruit and be disappointed with the results. The main reason for going after a major newspaper is that it has the power to provide some incredible leverage. If you can get press from a national newspaper, you can use this exposure to get press coverage from a small local paper. Many times, you won't even need to call them, because they'll call you. After all, they saw your article in the big paper.

Since getting featured in *Entrepreneur Magazine*, the *Vancouver Sun*, and the *National Post*, I have been asked to appear in several smaller publications as well, like the *Richmond News* and *Ming Pao Magazine*, which is written in Chinese! Yes, I've even crossed the language barrier.

Low-Cost Advertising

The traditional way to promote a website is through advertisements. These can include clickable banners, text link ads, and more. You might turn to services like Google AdWords and fork over some money so that you can buy some exposure on the Web. Done correctly, you can gain some visitors using this strategy, but not everyone has a boatload of cash to spend on advertising, especially if it's going to take a fair bit of experimentation to discover which advertising strategy works best. Promoting your blog doesn't have to cost a lot of money; I've covered some of inexpensive ways to promote your blog above. Pens and business cards are a good start in the offline world, but what about the online world? Can you get cheap online advertising?

Yes, you can.

The Ongoing Text Link Ad Promotion

Text Link Ads is an advertising network that serves up, you guessed it, text link ads on the Internet. These links can appear in the sidebars of many popular blogs and they offer post-level ads as well. It's paid advertising, but they've had a coupon code for as long as I can remember. When you are going through the checkout process, simply enter "starter kit" in the coupon code section and you will get $100 off! The caveat is that the total order must be at least $125, meaning that you will have to pony up $25 of your own money. Even so, you're getting $125 worth of advertising for just twenty-five bucks. If you're truly evil, you can even set up multiple accounts and use the same coupon over and over again. Better still, sign up as a TLA publisher and then refer yourself for an advertiser account! This way, you get the referral commission of $25, effectively making your net cost $0.00.

Sponsor a WordPress Theme

You may have noticed that when you look for free WordPress themes on the Web, many are sponsored. This sponsored link appears in the footer of the WordPress template, so anyone who downloads the free theme will also download that link intact. Thousands of bloggers use free popular WordPress themes, so by sponsoring one of these themes you get tons of backlinks from all around the blogosphere! Get in contact with the people who code these themes (look for contact information on the sites that offer free themes) and ask them how much they charge to embed your link in the footer. You'd be surprised by how little it can cost to get so many links. These might not help you with traffic directly, but they certainly don't hurt when it comes to search engine link juice.

Look Out for PPC Coupons

Always be on the lookout for these great coupons because they can offer you a lot of free advertising. From time to time, services like Google AdWords, Yahoo! Search Marketing, and Microsoft AdCenter will issue coupons to new customers. These can be up to $100 each and sometimes they are worth even more than that. I don't normally post about these coupons because they're in short supply and by the time I post about them, they may have already been used up. Just keep your eyes and ears peeled for these kinds of deals because you could score some serious advertising for basically no cost. I used a coupon for Microsoft AdCenter awhile ago for $200! Imagine if I were to set up five accounts using this coupon. I would effectively have enough to purchase $1,000 in free targeted, contextual ads. Imagine how much traffic that could bring.

Five Search Engine Optimization Action Items

Especially while your blog is relatively young, your focus should be on writing stellar content and then driving targeted traffic toward that content. You'll need to build up a loyal following of readers if you truly want to make money from a blog. If John Chow Dot Com did not have so many RSS subscribers, it would not have generated the level of traffic that it has and it would not have earned as much revenue as it has. One way that you can target traffic to your blog is through search engine optimization, or SEO, which helps your blog and the articles contained within to rank in Google and other search engines. Depending on your chosen niche, you will have different target keywords and keyword phrases. For example, I made quite the concerted effort to rank in Google for the term "make money online." Getting organic search engine results (also known as "natural" rankings, because they are not paid advertisements) for a term like that can be very valuable, especially since buying the sponsored links in the right sidebar of Google results—otherwise known as search engine marketing (SEM)—can be incredibly expensive.

As with Google AdWords campaigns, the cost of buying sidebar advertising space will vary based on the keyword or keyword phrase. The same can be said about the competition to get ranked for certain keywords in organic search results. The more competitive keywords will be much more difficult to crack, so when you are working on your search engine optimization, you may want to keep this in mind as well. For most blogs, one of the best strategies you can take is to focus your blog entries around a family of keywords and try to get other blogs to link to that content using the same keywords. For example, even though I went after "make money online", I kept my options open to related terms, like "make money blogging" and "making money online," among others.

Even though you should be writing your blog posts for your readers, there are still several things you can do to improve how those same articles rank in the search engines. The strategies described below are designed to help both your blog, and individual articles within your blog, achieve high Google rankings for targeted keyword searches.. Get people to your site any way you can, and then the goal is to keep them around with your stellar content.

1. Optimize Your Blog Post Titles

Think about the last time you looked for something in Google or some other search engine. In the results, you'd find a listing of what that search engine feels are the most relevant pages on the Internet related to your search term. Each time your keyword appears—both in the title of the page and the brief snippet shown underneath—it appears in bold, highlighting the relative relevancy of the search results. One of the factors that these search engines use to determine the content (and thus, the relevancy) of your post is its title. The title that you give your blog post can mean the difference between getting a visitor from Google and getting buried so far down in the search results that no one is ever going to find you.

Yes, you want to be dynamic with your blog post titles, but if you want them to rank well in Google, you'll also need to be descriptive. If you're writing a post about the best burger you've ever eaten, it's perfectly acceptable to title it "The Best Burger I've Ever Eaten." In contrast, a title like "Inhaling a Pound of Flesh" is more creative and might grab the attention of existing readers. The actual content of the post can be identical, but you can see how these two different post titles would have very different results (and elicit very different reactions). The trouble with being very descriptive with your blog post titles, especially if you start getting into the habit of keyword stuffing, is that the titles will come out sounding a little generic.

It's a delicate balance, to be sure, but keeping those keywords in mind when writing the titles of your blog posts is very important. In the example described in the previous paragraph, you could easily get away with either of those titles. The worst thing you can do is come up with a title that is neither captivating nor descriptive. Say that you decided to title that post "Lunch with Mom." Existing readers will probably think it's going to be a boring post, and the search engines will not necessarily associate your post with the keyword phrase "best burger." The ideal is to have an interesting title that also happens to be descriptive. Perhaps "Spending $100 on the Best Burger in Town" is a better option.

2. Recognize the Importance of the First Paragraph

In addition to optimizing your blog post title, it's also important that you pay attention to keywords and keyword phrases in the first paragraph of each blog post, particularly in the first sentence.

As part of my concerted effort to rank well for the phrase "make money online," I made it a point to include that exact phrase in just about every relevant blog post I wrote. While it's true that the Google bot will spider through most of your content to understand its subject matter, there is more weight placed near the beginning of an article because this is typically where the main topic is laid out and discussed.

On a related note, the first paragraph also sets the tone for the rest of the article. When you skim through a newspaper, what is the usual routine? You pan your eyes across the pages to see if there are any interesting headlines or images. If an image or headline catches your eye, you may be inclined to read the first sentence or first paragraph of the article. Guess what? Most Web users do the same thing when they are looking for something to read on the Internet. If and when they come across one of your blog entries, they'll read the title first to see if it's relevant to their interests. Getting past this first barrier, they'll then move on to the first couple of sentences. It is here that you really need to capture their attention and get them to read further. The goal is to get them to read your whole article, after all.

3. Never Forget the ALT and TITLE Tags in Images

They say that a picture is worth a thousand words, but Google doesn't think so. As powerful as their search engine algorithm may be, they're not the best at figuring out what your photos are all about. We all know that including relevant pictures in our posts can serve several positive purposes. Why just talk about your lunch when you can include a picture of it? Why just talk about the new leash you got for your dog when you can show everyone what it looks like? These pictures, when used correctly, add great value to the user experience, and they can encourage site visitors to stick around, subscribe to your RSS feed, and read every one of your posts.

When most people think about search engine optimization, they only consider getting ranked for the content itself. This is a very narrow-minded view. You've probably noticed that Google also has an Image Search function that people can use to search specifically for images. This can also be an incredible source of traffic to your blog because if someone is looking for a picture of a Ferrari, they might be in interested in your blog about Italian supercars. If they're looking for a picture of a stylish Nokia Smartphone, they're probably interested in your blog about high-end mobile phones. When a user clicks on one of the image results, they are sent to the page that contains that image.

There are a few key strategies that you can deploy to ensure that Google knows exactly what your pictures are about. First, make sure that the file name of the image is descriptive. When you take a picture with a digital camera, you probably end up with a file name similar to DSC-0304.JPG or something, right? If you were to look at only the file name, you would have no idea about the content of the picture. Now imagine if you renamed that picture greasyburger.jpg. Wow! That's a lot more descriptive!

Second, when you upload the image to your blog, be sure to fill in both the ALT and TITLE tags. The WordPress upload tool should offer these fields to you when you upload a new picture, so you'll want to include some sort of short description in both of those fields. If not, you can also enter them manually by looking at the code and doing something similar to this:

<img src='http://www.example.com/greasyburger.jpg' alt='here is a greasy burger' title='a hamburger with a lot of grease'>

This tells Google Image Search a little more about what's in the picture and, thus, will help your blog improve its ranking when someone happens to search for a picture of a greasy burger.

Third, the content around the picture should be related to the picture. If you actually write about the greasy burger in both the paragraph preceding and following the picture of the greasy burger, this will also help your cause. This shows that the photo is relevant and that the surrounding information is related to the picture itself.

4. Install the All in One SEO Pack for WordPress

Wouldn't it be nice if there was a fancy WordPress plug-in that would help you with all your search engine optimization needs? Wouldn't it be nice if there was a plug-in that would help you to handle things like meta tags and search engine optimized titles? Thankfully, there is. The appropriately named All in One SEO Pack allows you to control the title, description, and keyword META tags for every post you write on your blog. Typically, when you write a blog post, Google will look to the actual title for the title, it will pull the first paragraph as the description, and it will leave your META tags empty. With the All in One SEO Pack, you can optimize all of this yourself.

Perhaps the All in One SEO Pack's coolest feature is that it allows you to have two titles for a single blog post. Remember how I said that blog post titles are very important and how you should focus on getting them to be both captivating to a human reader and descriptive enough for the search engines? The All in One SEO Pack lets you satisfy both needs. When setting the title for your post, you can write the more intriguing one as the actual title. In the All in One SEO Pack dialog that fits underneath the area where you compose the blog post itself, you can then set a more search engine optimized title. This title appears in the top of web browsers, and it is also the title that appears in the search engine results page (SERP).

Beyond the individual settings you'll be able to select for each post, this plug-in grants you control over several key elements on your home page, which happens to be your blog's most important page. After installing and activating the All in One SEO Pack, you'll find its settings under the "Options" section of the WordPress control panel. From here, you are able to set a home page title, description, and keywords *that are independent of any other option.* Having an effective home page title can work wonders for your search engine performance, because it can ultimately be much more descriptive than just the name of your blog. Having a title like "Making Money Online with John Chow Dot Com" is more useful than having a title like "John Chow Dot Com".

It also lets you front-load the keywords rather than have them trail off in the distance. Depending on the WordPress theme you are using, you may need to edit your header.php file to remove the meta keyword and description call tags (these contain information that tell search engines about the content of the post). Otherwise, you may end up with two sets of meta keyword and description per page.

The All in One SEO Pack also allows you to exclude duplicate content, like the archives and categories, from your blog's indexing. As mentioned before, Google will penalize you for duplicate content *even if it's your own.* When you write an individual blog post, it does not exist in isolation. It can be found in your main archives section, which is automatically generated by WordPress, and it can also be found under the associated blog post category. This duplicates the content and can dilute the value of your article in Google's eyes. By excluding the duplicate content, you are giving search engines a more accurate portrayal of the content of your blog.

In a nutshell, the All in One SEO Pack makes your blog and the posts contained within a lot more search engine friendly. The plug-in won't guarantee that you'll rank for your target keywords and keyword phrases, but it certainly helps.

5. Don't Forget About Internal Deeplinking

I touched on this topic in an earlier chapter, but it's worth reiterating because deeplinking to your own articles is very important to search engine optimization. The number of links pointing toward a page is one of the most crucial factors that Google uses to determine the relative importance of a web page. Going even further than that, Google also looks at the anchor text used to link to that web page. Think about that for a moment. When most people link to the home page of Microsoft, there is a good chance that they are linking to it using the term "Microsoft" as the clickable text (otherwise known as anchor text). This is part of the reason why the Microsoft home page ranks first for the search term "Microsoft."

The interesting thing is that while links from external sites are the ones that add the most value, the internal links are the ones that can help define the content of a web page, which helps Google to understand what the page is about. You should be deeplinking to your old articles on a regular basis, keeping your target keywords and keyword phrases in mind when doing so. Do not link to your old posts using the anchor text "click here." That's not useful.

Chapter Nine:
The Importance of Branding

In this chapter, we'll take a look at what it means to establish a brand, and why branding is so critical to your blog's success.

If you want to make money from a blog, you need to treat it as if it were a business like any other. Marketing experts constantly remind retailers and other companies about the importance of branding. To be truly successful, you need to separate yourself from your competition, and stand out from the crowd in such a way that all your potential customers-or site visitors in the case of a commercial blog—can instantly recognize your brand.

When people see that distinctive swoosh, they immediately think of Nike. That's brand power. When people hear that characteristic song, they are immediately reminded of Apple and the Mac vs. PC series of commercials. You want to achieve this same level of brand recognition with your blog. Certain company slogans and logos are ingrained into our very beings, which is the result of a purposeful effort by their respective marketing teams. We see a blue oval and we think of Ford. We catch a glimpse of the golden arches and we begin to salivate over McDonald's fries. Your blog should be no exception.

In order to separate yourself from the millions of blogs in the blogosphere, you need to create your own brand. When you have a brand, you have a huge advantage over the generic blog next door. Think about it. If a well-branded blog writes about the exact same topic as some other blog that just blends in with all the rest on the Internet, there's a very good chance that the well-branded blog will get more press and more attention. The Nintendo Wii, for instance, makes use of existing gyroscopic motion-sensing technology. Even so, because Nintendo has such a strong brand presence, they got a lot of attention for the revolutionary control scheme. When no-name companies tried to do the same thing, no one noticed. Are you familiar with the hundreds of cell phone manufacturers in China? Probably not, but you do know about Nokia and Samsung. Brand power goes a long way.

So, how do you go about establishing a brand for your blog?

It Starts with the Domain Name

When a lot of amateurs first dive into the world of blogs, they seem to hesitate to get their own domain names. This never ceases to amaze me because if you're serious about making money from a blog, you cannot do it without your own domain. You cannot build a brand without one. For this reason, if you've decided to enter blogging with a free account on blogspot.com or wordpress.com, it's time for you to get out and invest in your own domain. You can register a domain name for less than $10 and you can host it for only a few dollars per month. This is a very minimal investment to build your brand.

When you host your blog at a free service like blogspot.com, you are not building your brand; you are building the brand of Blogspot. com. It makes a lot more sense to start out with your own domain from the beginning because if you start with a free service and move later on, you're just going to lose all the hard work that you've put into the blog. You'll lose all of the backlinks that you've accumulated, and you'll no longer reap the rewards of your search engine optimization efforts. By moving from a free service to your own domain, you're essentially starting from scratch. You can avoid this wasted effort by investing ten bucks into your brand with a personalized domain name.

Your domain will serve as a primary focal point for the branding of your blog. It is in your best interest to spend some time thinking about what your domain will be because this is something that will stick with your blog in the long run. Other elements, like the layout and logo, may change over time, but you want to keep the same domain over the long haul. It's all about branding. You don't want someone to get used to reading http://www.johnchow.com, only to discover the next day that the blog has been moved to http://www.internetmogul.com.

When choosing the domain for your blog, keep the following three points in mind.

1. Make It Memorable and Make It Unique

You may only have a handful of opportunities to capture a potential reader, so it's important that you choose a domain that is not only easy to remember, but also one that is distinctly different from all the other blogs on the Internet. In essence, there are three core strategies that you can consider when deciding on a unique domain name.

The first strategy is to find a domain that is actually descriptive. When I got around to launching my technology website, I decided on http://www.thetechzone.com because it described exactly what the site was all about. It's a zone that is filled with the latest technology. Even though the components that make up the domain are everyday words, the combination of them is brandable and unique. Similarly, you could look at the website of someone like Darren Rowse, who runs http://www.problogger.net. This domain describes exactly what he does and what the site is about: professional blogging. The trouble with trying to get a traditional, descriptive domain name is that many of the good ones have already been taken. You may have to do a fair bit of trial and error before you find a domain that is available and brandable. There are two key advantages to using a descriptive domain name: readers know exactly what to expect, and you also get some SEO benefits for your target keywords.

The second strategy is to come up with a completely original word, or one that has not yet been used in the context of the Internet. Some of the best examples of this are websites like Google, Digg, and Woot. The words are essentially nonsensical, but for whatever reason, they are incredibly memorable. Given the right marketing techniques, you can brand such a domain very well. The examples above aren't blogs, but you can see how this strategy could apply to the blogosphere. The advantage to using a completely original word is that you are working with a blank slate: readers will not have any preconceived notions about what your site should offer. This also means that you're free to brand your blog however you see fit. In the off-line world, you see this technique used by companies like Adobe, Sony, and Ferrari. It's also possible to use something that already exists. Nike did this with the Greek goddess of triumph.

The third strategy is a combination of the first two strategies. You can see this technique employed by popular technology blogs like Engadget and Gizmodo. They have created truly original names that are highly brandable, but their domains contain a very descriptive element. Engadget talks about gadgets and Gizmodo talks about gizmos. In many ways, this technique can offer the best of both worlds: you get an accurate description of the blog's subject matter, but also get an original name that can be branded from the get-go.

2. Don't Use Your Name for a Commercial Blog

This might sound a little counter-intuitive since I'm best known for being the blogger behind John Chow Dot Com, but if you plan on running a commercial blog that makes money online, you really shouldn't use your own name for the domain. This was the advice that I gave to Scott Wainner when he approached me with this very question. He owned the domain to his name, but I advised him to use a different domain instead. He ultimately decided on http://www.wrevenue.com. But why did I go with http://www.johnchow.com/?

Well, the original goal of my blog was not to make money. My original intention was to use it as a personal blog where I could talk about whatever was on my mind. Most of my early readers were just friends and family members, and the blog served as a way for them to keep up with what was happening in my life. It was not supposed to be a commercial operation, but when I started the case study to determine whether or not I could make money from a personal blog, the priorities started to change. The blog became commercial.

If I had decided from the beginning that my blog was going to become a commercial operation, I would not have selected http:// www.johnchow.com as the domain. It would have made more sense to create a new blog that focused on making money online, keeping http://www.johnchow.com as my domain for a personal blog. This is largely because it's much easier to brand a commercial name than it is to brand your own name. Your marketing efforts are easier when you try to brand something like Apple and Microsoft rather than Steve Jobs and Bill Gates. For the average blogger, branding your own name is extremely difficult. I had the advantage of already being known in tech circles, but this advantage is not available to most people who are just starting out.

As much as you would like to make money from blogging, there may come a time when you want to sell the site. Engadget was originally an independent operation, but then it was purchased by Weblogs, Inc. When your domain is your own name, the site becomes impossible to sell. Weblogs, Inc. would not have purchased the site if its domain was http://www.ryanblock.com. There would be no reason for someone to purchase John Chow Dot Com unless they planned on keeping me around to update the site, which defeats the purpose. If I want to sell a blog, I want to cash out and leave. I don't want to stick around and work for someone else!

The other trouble with using your own name as your domain is that readers expect you to produce most, if not all, of the content. When people come to John Chow Dot Com, they expect to read something written by John Chow. In contrast, if they were to go to something like http://www. makemoneyonline.com, they would just expect to read something about making money online and not necessarily something from one specific author. If you have a commercial name for your blog, you have a lot more freedom in terms of getting other writers to produce the content.

You should definitely register your own name as a domain name, but don't use it for commercial purposes.

3. Avoid Any Ambiguity about Spelling

In trying to come up with an original domain name for your blog, you may start to get a little creative with how it's spelled. Sure, spelling a common word uniquely could work wonders for branding, but it may ultimately work against you. After all, what's the point of having a great name for your blog if no one can find it? When you purposely misspell something for effect, people may have trouble remembering the unique spelling. There are blogs out there that have decided to be hip and cool by replacing an "s" with a "z," for example, but that just makes them forgettable. Imagine if I decided to use http://www.thatekzone.com instead of http://www.thetechzone.com. Yes, it could be hip and trendy, but people are going to have trouble remembering it.

This applies not only to words that have been misspelled on purpose, but also to words that may be difficult to spell in general, or words that could have multiple spellings. For example, a graphic artist may want a domain like colorwheel.com. The problem with this is that it could also be spelled colourwheel.com, and if you hope to have any sort of international success, you need to choose words that are spelled only one way. Alternatively, you can buy all the alternative spellings and have them redirect to your domain.

The best domains are those that are memorable and easy to spell. Some of the most popular blogs make use of this strategy—TechCrunch, Lifehacker, Shoemoney, etc.—because there is no way that you would spell those domains incorrectly. There are very few sites that have managed to achieve success with typos, and perhaps one of the most notable is a spoof of my own blog, called John Cow Dot Com. He took my concept of "make money online" and put a bovine spin on it, telling people how to make "mooney" online. Sites like these are few and far between.

You Need a Custom Logo

It's hard to stand out from the crowd, and that's why branding is so important. When you are first starting out with your blog, most people aren't going to know who you are. Moreover, most people have a lot of trouble connecting a name with a face unless they make quite a bit of an effort to do so. Needless to say, most visitors to your blog are not going to make that effort to remember you. The onus is on you to be as memorable and recognizable as possible.

This is why you need a custom logo. All the big, brand-name products in the world have logos. Successful logos are distinctive and automatically associated with the appropriate product or organization. When people see that stylized eye, they think of CBS. When people see those three stripes, they immediately associate them with Adidas. Happen to come across a three-pronged circle? You're probably already thinking of Mercedes. Part of the branding strategy for your blog should involve a logo.

Jeremy Schoemaker, known to most people simply as Shoemoney, is one of the better known bloggers on the Internet, but the vast majority of people would have a hard time picking his face out of a lineup. Most people cannot connect his face with his blog. However, once they see that distinctive dollar sign-like logo, they know who he is. Looking around the rest of the blogosphere, you will find other great logos that have built up a lot of brand recognition online. Another great example is Super Affiliate Zac Johnson, whose logo is a funny caricature of himself. It's distinctive and memorable. He's even gone so far as to create a custom bobblehead doll!

If you have a good eye for design, it's possible to create your own custom logo for your blog, but it's probably better to elicit the services of a professional. It doesn't have to be expensive, though. While the higher-end professionals can cost a pretty penny, most bloggers can get away with soliciting the services of a freelancer on sites like the Digital Point forums. Depending on who you hire, you may be able to get an original, Web 2.0-friendly logo for about $10. Better still, most will create a few for you to choose from, based on your preferences and specifications. When in doubt, keep it simple. You will likely want to use the logo on promotional products like business cards, pens, T-shirts, and other items.

I didn't have a logo for John Chow Dot Com when I first started the blog. I have no doubt that using a logo from the start would have helped me to brand the blog. Thankfully, I had the added advantage of already being known in tech circles, so my name was already a preexisting brand. It was a brand that had to extend beyond the world of "just" technology and into the world of making money through blogging.

Time for a Unique Blog Design

Having a great custom logo is one thing, but if your blog looks the same as the millions of other blogs on the Internet, it's still going to be very difficult to stick out and get noticed. When I first launched John Chow Dot Com, I made use of a free WordPress template. This is because John Chow Dot Com was going to be little more than a personal blog for my friends and family. As the focus on the blog shifted to something more commercial, I needed a new, unique theme to reflect that shift.

It's far too hard to build a brand when you look like everyone else. The beauty of WordPress is that is you do not necessarily need to invest in a completely custom theme. When you get a free WordPress theme from any number of sources online, you should not use the template right out of the box. If you do this, then your blog will look like every other blog that uses that same theme. Even though the original John Chow Dot Com used the free MistyLook theme, I made it stand out by altering several elements. It was still similar to other MistyLook-powered blogs, but it was different enough to be distinctive.

I changed around the colors and, more importantly, added my own custom header image. Having a custom header image, especially one that makes use of your custom logo, can go a long way in developing your brand and getting it recognized on the Web. Displaying the name of your blog at the top in some generic font is not enough; you also need to express some individuality through your header image. Ironically, because the MistyLook theme became associated with me, anyone else running it was called a copycat.

Ideally, you'll want to create a completely new custom theme that is unlike any other on the Web. John Chow Dot Com received a major overhaul in August 2007. I used the service offered by Nate Whitehill and Unique Blog Designs for this purpose, and they designed a new theme specifically to maximize advertising revenue. The free MistyLook theme had limited potential for making money, so I got Nate to make a theme that had advertising in mind from the get-go. He made room for additional ad spaces without detracting from the user experience. That's critical. If the ad spaces detract too much from the user experience, you run the risk of losing your readers and, in the end, if you lose readers, you'll probably lose money too.

Using a completely custom theme will work wonders at getting your blog to stand out in a way that can't be achieved simply by providing original content and slapping on a custom header image. Many bloggers often underestimate the importance of a good design; readers need to have a visual sense of your blog as distinctive and unique. They're much more likely to come back if the design is memorable. Can you see Google's home page in your head? Can you see the Apple home page in your mind's eye? That's the power of great design. You want to achieve the same level of enduring appeal with your blog.

Have a Great "About" Page

When someone arrives at your blog for the first time, they really have no idea what to expect. They probably don't know who you are or why they should care what you have to say. After reading some of your fantastic content, they might be a little more interested in your blog and they'll want to find out more. This is where your "About" page comes into play.

The "About" page is the blogging equivalent of a résumé. When you apply for a job, your résumé represents all your qualifications and shows them in the best possible light. You feature the experience you have to offer to the company, telling the employer exactly why you are a better applicant than the other guy in the waiting room. When it comes to your blog, it isn't all that different. You are vying for the attention of readers and when they subscribe, revisiting your website on a regular basis, you could say that you've been "hired."

It's common knowledge that many people embellish the contents of their résumé, downplaying (or omitting) the negative stuff and focusing on the positive. An "About" page is much the same and it gives you an opportunity to really shine. It lets you express your personality and tell all your readers what the blog is about and why they should come back. This also helps to build your brand.

One of the most critical elements of "About" page is a photo of the blogger(s) behind the site. Having a picture on the page helps to connect readers with your blog because it shows that you are a real person and not just words on a computer screen. This builds trust and, in turn, does a lot in establishing and maintaining your brand. It also helps, of course, to tell people a little bit about yourself and how the blog came to be. If your blog uses multiple writers, you can have sections on the "About" page for the blog and for each of the bloggers.

If you want to see a great "About" page, check out the one made by Timothy Ferriss, author of *The 4-Hour Workweek*. Tim's "About" page is designed to establish him as an authority on his subject—escaping the nine-to-five and being a more efficient person—and it does a great job of highlighting his accomplishments. Readers automatically respect him because he is honest and his accomplishments are formidable. To control his brand, Tim offers official press photos for both his book and himself. It might be worthwhile to invest in official press photos so that you can avoid other people writing with photos that aren't so nice. You want them to write about you and your blog, but unflattering pictures are probably not so good.

What Makes You Different From Everyone Else?

This is the question you're going to have to ask yourself if you want your blog to succeed. Why would someone want to read your blog instead of another blog offering similar content? What makes you so special? This conundrum is at the very core of branding. You need to find something that makes you different, something that makes you special. From fast food restaurants to clothing lines, companies find a certain aspect or characteristic element that they can own and call their own. A blog (and blogger) is no different.

There are countless other blogs on the Internet that talk about making money online, but John Chow Dot Com is different. I've come to be known as the "root of all evil," and this plays an integral part of the branding for the blog. Unlike other blogs, John Chow Dot Com has an edge; I'm not afraid to talk about marketing and money-making strategies that are considered black hat, or a little on the evil side of things. For example, I've already suggested that you to sign up for two separate accounts with an advertising network just so that you can refer yourself and earn the referral commission. That's pretty evil, and it's not the type of advice that you may find on a more conventional online money-making blog. I'm not saying that you should try to be evil too, but you should have a certain voice or characteristic that sets you apart from other blogs in your niche.

Another person that you can look to for branding inspiration is Robert Kiyosaki. His last name is pretty hard to remember, so that's why he created a truly original brand that is not only memorable, but also very descriptive and unique. You might know Kiyosaki better as the Rich Dad. He's written a series of books and runs a series of conferences as well, many of which he doesn't even need to attend himself! His brand has enough power that he can just send representatives on his behalf, selling his message, his brand, and his methodologies.

Building your brand is one of the most important components to having a successful blog. The last thing you want to be is generic and boring. Be memorable.

Chapter Ten:
Optimizing Google AdSense

In this chapter, we'll talk about how you can make the most money possible from Google AdSense, one of the Internet's most popular advertising platforms.

Don't put all your eggs in one basket. I've always adhered to this philosophy, and it applies to just about every aspect of blogging too. Even so, when most people first start out with a blog, they will inevitably sign up with Google AdSense because it's probably the biggest advertising network out there. It also helps that they have a very low barrier to entry, which is in sharp contrast to some other advertising networks that have much more stringent requirements for their applicants. With AdSense, all you need is a website.

In the long run, you should not rely solely on Google AdSense for monetizing your blog. If I only used AdSense for John Chow Dot Com, I would have maxed out at only a few thousand dollars a month rather than continuing to grow with alternative income streams until I was able to make over $30,000 a month. Even so, AdSense is a great place to start, and I recommend that you go with AdSense in the beginning, complementing it with other advertising techniques as your blog continues to grow.

The Google AdSense Paradigm

A common misconception among blogging outsiders is that all you have to do is set up a generic blog, throw up some Google AdSense ads, and just wait for the checks to arrive in the mail. The fact of the matter is that it's not quite this easy. Even if you've managed to build up a decent readership and your traffic numbers are increasing, this does not necessarily mean that you'll automatically start making money from Google.

As I mentioned in chapter 2, Google AdSense may have single-handedly saved the Internet. It brought advertising opportunities back to the masses. The difference, however, was that with Google, the income was not directly proportional to traffic numbers. Ads in the pre-AdSense era were predominantly based on the CPM model, which means that a certain amount of money would be paid per thousand ad impressions. It didn't matter if someone clicked on the ad or even paid attention to the banner; the publisher would get paid just the same. This is not the case with Google AdSense. A visitor to your site needs to click on the ad in order for you to get paid, and that's why you need to optimize the ad placements. You want to maximize your click-thru rate (CTR).

Yes, having lots of traffic is important, but maximizing your monetization from that traffic is even more important. Many people have wondered how is it possible that John Chow Dot Com makes in excess of $30,000 a month. While traffic steadily increased during 2007 and 2008, the income growth was not proportional to traffic growth; it far surpassed it. Traffic may double, for example, but I grew the income by much more than double. Ad optimization is key.

The Easiest Way to Add AdSense to a Blog

If your blog is powered by WordPress, as I recommended, then it's actually very easy to add Google AdSense to your blog. One of the most common questions that I get from readers is how to set up Google AdSense ads on a blog. This comes up a lot because the general public seems to be familiar with AdSense, and they assume that it's a good tool for making money with blogs. Amateurs, when they are first starting out, may assume that they need to insert the generated AdSense code into each and every post. This can be a repetitive and ultimately useless practice. Worst still, it could violate the AdSense Terms of Service, because you're not allowed to have more than three AdSense ad units displayed at any given time.

How, then, can you implement the ad units without having to copy and paste the code each time? How do you adhere to the Terms of Service, limiting the number of ad units to three per page? By far the easiest and simplest way to add AdSense to a blog is the AdSense Deluxe WordPress plug-in. The great thing about this plug-in is that it will only show three ad units on the home page, but when you click on any of the individual posts, it will be able to display the ad on that page as well. This is a great solution, particularly for people who use the inline 300x250 pixel rectangle ad creative. The term "ad creative" refers to the design and content of an advertisement. This is the ad size that I used on John Chow Dot Com. I right-aligned the ad unit and wrapped the first paragraph around it.

The AdSense Deluxe WordPress plug-in, despite its name, will actually work with a wide range of advertising networks, including the Yahoo! Publisher Network (YPN) as well as private ad sales. Installation and implementation of the plug-in is reasonably straightforward. After downloading the file, you simply unzip it and then upload it to the plug-ins folder on your WordPress blog. From there, you go to the WordPress dashboard to activate the plug-in; there, you can customize it through the Options panel. It sounds more complicated than it is. Another great thing about the plug-in is that it is able to manage multiple ad sizes. Maybe you don't want to use the inline 300 pixel box on every post, and prefer to use a 468x60 pixel banner instead, for certain articles. All you have to do is use the different call code associated with the other ad creative.

The AdSense block that you choose as the default can be called upon when you write a post by using the code <!--adsense--> whereas if you want to call upon the ad unit that you labeled as banner, then you use the call code <!--adsense#banner-->. Another common question that people have about implementing AdSense into your blog is how to do the text wraparound for the 300 pixel box. To do this, simply wrap the AdSense call code with a division align code. I align the box to the right, so the code is:

<!--adsense-->

If you want to align the ad box to the left, simply swap out the "float:right" with "float:left." That's obvious enough. Although I typically embed the ad code near the top of the post, other bloggers have found more success from placing the code a little further down the post. Your mileage will vary, so it is best to do a little experimentation to see which ad placement works best. While the easiest way to implement the ad code is to edit it right into the index.php file of the theme template (and the single.php or post.php files as well), I don't recommend that you do this because you may not want to place a Google AdSense ad unit in certain posts. An exception might be something like the 468x60 p banner that you can use at the bottom of every post. You will need to familiarize yourself somewhat with PHP when doing this.

The plug-in will keep track of the number of AdSense ads running on a page, and it will limit the number displayed to three. This will ensure that you adhere to AdSense's Terms of Service. Another nice feature of AdSense Deluxe is its ability to globally enable and disable ads. This also means that if you choose to change the color scheme of your blog at some point in the future, you can just edit the ad unit within the AdSense Deluxe plug-in and it will change how the ads appear on every post where you used the code. Contrast this to the amount of work you'd need to do to manually edit each and every post. This is a huge time-saver!

Understanding the Google AdSense Bid System

The Google AdSense system, in many ways, is tied to the Google search system. When you go to Google to look for something, you type in a certain term, right? These terms are known as keywords and keyword phrases, and it is in your best interest to understand how these work if you want to make money from a blog. When someone purchases advertising through Google AdWords (the "buying" side of Google AdSense), they typically bid on a chosen keyword or keyword phrase. Let's say, for example, that they bid on the keyword "puppies." They tell Google how much they would like to pay for each ad click, also providing Google with a daily budget that should not be exceeded. By placing a bid, the advertiser does not guarantee that their ad will be shown on any given website. This is because they are effectively competing against every other advertiser who has bid on the same keyword: "puppies," in this instance.

Make Money with AdSense

Now, let's move over to the publisher side of things. That's the side that you need to be interested in if you want to make money from Google AdSense. When you write a blog post, Google will spider through your content to determine the subject matter. If you happened to write an article and Google decides to apply the keyword "puppies" to your post, the AdSense ads served on that page will reflect that content. This is known as contextual advertising, because the ads shown depended on the content of the page. The Google spider may not figure out your content immediately, but assuming that your site is indexed, Google will get to it eventually. The more important your blog is, the more often it will be spidered by Google. As you can imagine, the spider bot makes its way through CNN.com much more often than the never-visited blog of Joe Public.

Moreover, as you can imagine, certain keywords are more popular than others. Advertisers are willing to spend more money on a keyword phrase like "credit cards" than they would be willing to spend on a keyword phrase like "pink platypus". In this way, many bloggers target certain keywords with the goal of making more money from Google AdSense. This is a perfectly acceptable strategy, so long as you still focus on providing quality content for your readers and the ads don't detract from the user experience.

Another important aspect of the Google AdSense system is something called the Google Bid Gap.

The Gap Spans the Great Divide

In a nutshell, the bid gap is simply the difference in price between Google ads. When you place a 300x250 pixel ad box in your blog, for example, it will typically display four advertisements, each linking to a different advertiser associated with a relevant keyword or keyword phrase. The advertiser who placed the largest bid will get the top spot, whereas the advertiser who placed the second largest bid gets the second spot, and so on. The gaps between the top four bids are typically very close, because the advertisers are vying to get as close to the top spot as possible without spending too much money. For example, the bids on a high-paying keyword could be as much as $5.00, $4.99, $4.97, and $4.95. If the second advertiser increased his bid to $5.01, he would effectively take over the top spot.

From a publisher's point of view, this means that it won't make that much of a difference whether a site visitor clicks on the first ad or the fourth ad. This will vary depending on the keyword and how the market is going at the time, of course. Your goal is still to get site visitors to click on the ads so that you can make some money. The higher the payout level and the higher the click-thru rate, the more money you'll be making. This is calculated as your eCPM, or effective cost per thousand page impressions.

Where the bid gap starts to get a lot bigger is when you compare position four with position five. Continuing with our previous example, the fourth advertiser may have put in a bid of $4.95, but the advertiser who ranks in fifth place may have only put in a bid for 10 cents. This might sound like an exaggeration, but it's not out of the ordinary to find such large gaps with the highest-paying keywords. Also bear in mind that the bid gap can also be dependent on the ad creative.

Advertisers that bid on the 300×250 p box may not bid on the 468×60 pixel banner, for example. In any case, the gap between bids four and five could have a drastic effect on your income.

Remember how I said that you can run a maximum of three Google AdSense ad units on a single page? If you loaded up your article with these three ad units, assuming you got the same keyword that these advertisers are targeting, you would effectively get one ad unit with four high-paying advertisers, and then two ad units below that with eight low-paying advertisers. Because there are twelve advertisers on one single post, there is a very good chance that a site visitor may click on one of the lower-paying ads. You're giving them the option to leave your website for only a couple of pennies. In this kind of situation, it would be in your best interest to reduce the number of Google ads to get rid of the gigantic bid gap. By only displaying the ads that pay the most, you increase the chance that a site visitor will click on one of these ads. It sounds a little counter-intuitive, but it is absolutely true.

AdWords advertisers know that most Google ad sizes display a maximum of four ads, so they compete furiously to get within the first four spots. This is because they know that many sites will only run one AdSense unit on a page. Bids on the second set of four could be substantially lower, because the advertisers know that they will have a smaller chance of being displayed. There are still some quality advertisers in this second set, of course, but they're also the ones that can't afford to get into the first set. When it comes to the third set of four—positions nine through twelve—these spots are typically where you find MFA (Made for AdSense) sites. Needless to say, these ad spots usually pay only a couple of pennies.

Can Less Be More?
Generally speaking, you will need to find the right number of ads to display on your particular blog. That number may also vary from article to article. When you increase the number of ad spots, you are always opening up the door for a lot of low-paying

advertisements. When you reduce the number of ad spots, you will likely see a significant decrease in the sheer number of clicks. This is because there are fewer ads displayed on the page, so it's less likely that a visitor will click on the ad. You will have to monitor your ad performance to make sure the total revenue continues to go up when you reduce the number of AdSense ads on a page. It's a very delicate balance, but you'll find that when the bid gap is big, revenue will increase as you reduce ads. If the bid gap isn't as big, if the difference between spot one and spot eight isn't so big, you might make more money with more ads. You'll just have to keep an eye on things. Don't be afraid to experiment.

Unfortunately, there is no explicit way for you to find out exactly what the bid gap is for a certain keyword or keyword phrase. Google does not release this information. In order for you to keep track of how your specific ads are doing, you can set up custom channels in the Google AdSense system for each ad unit. You can then see their stats individually and monitor the number of clicks and the amount of money that it is making. If the eCPM of one ad unit is significantly greater than another unit with a similar click-thru rate, then this is an indication of a big bid gap. Remove the ad with the lower eCPM and see if your overall revenue increases. If the people who were clicking on the lower paying ads start clicking on the higher paying ads, then it means that your overall revenue will start to improve. If the bid gap is big enough, the difference in click value will make up for the loss of clicks from the lower-paying ad unit.

Section Targeting

Section targeting is probably one of the least-known aspects of trying to make money from a blog, particularly from Google AdSense. It's a resource that many bloggers don't even know about, but it could work to drastically increase their income. If you want to make some serious cash from AdSense, you should think about section targeting and use it on a regular basis.

In a nutshell, section targeting helps to tell Google exactly what your blog article is all about. You may have noticed that when you write certain posts, Google doesn't provide you with the most well-targeted contextual ads. You might be writing about puppies, for example, but the AdSense ads that show up on your blog are promoting video games. What gives? Well, with section targeting, you help to point Google toward the specific content that more accurately reveals what the entire article is about. The reason you may be getting unrelated ads on your blog is that the content isn't targeted enough for the keyword or keyword phrases that you are trying to attract. Google tries its best to figure out what you're writing about, but it doesn't always succeed.

By using section targeting, you are isolating certain portions of your content that you want Google to focus on for the purpose of determining what ads should be served on your website. The Google spider will likely still look at the rest of the content, but the section that you recommend to them will be emphasized, and the ads will largely be related to the content contained within this recommended section. In other words, instead spidering the entire page to determine what ads should be served on your web page, Google will pay closer attention to the sections you target, while largely ignoring the sections that you don't target.

Using this strategy is actually very easy and is comprised of a single opening and single closing tag:

<!--google_ad_section_start-->

Here is a section of text that I want Google to pay attention to, because this is where I talk about puppies, and I want the ads served to be about dogs, canines, and man's best friend. Fido is a puppy, and he is my favorite pet, because he is a dog. I can start to stack the keywords here, like dogs, dog breeds, dog food, puppies, Puppy Chow, dog training, puppy training, and puppy food. This section is all about dogs and puppies, so the ads will probably be about dogs and puppies.

<!--google_ad_section_end-->

All the content contained within the two tags will then be targeted by Google, and the AdSense ads being served on that page will largely be determined by this highlighted section of text, rather than the rest of the page. If the rest of the article is not as keyword rich and veers off-topic on several occasions, AdSense may have a hard time assigning the most relevant ads. By using section targeting, as in the example above, Google will know to show ads about dogs and puppies.

An equivalent and opposite strategy is to tell Google what sections to explicitly ignore. This reverse targeting may be more effective if you stay on topic more often than not, because you can then tell Google to downplay the portions that aren't on topic. The ignore tags are like this:

<!--google_ad_section_start(weight=ignore)-->
Ignore this section, because it is completely off-topic, talking about
TV shows, cats, backpacks, and finding cheap hotels in London.
<!--google_ad_section_end(weight=ignore)-->

If you have ads popping up on your blog that don't have anything to do with the content, it could be due to a small paragraph that's throwing the Google spider into a tailspin. By telling the spider to ignore this paragraph, you'll get more well-targeted ads, which will increase the chances that your visitors will click on them.. After all, if someone is reading about puppies, they are probably more interested in ads that are also about puppies. Section targeting should be a key component to your strategy to make money online. While you want to largely stick within your niche and area of interest for the vast majority of your blog, you are able to go off-topic and ramble a little if you make good use of the Google section targeting, particularly the ignore variant.

Competitive Ad Filter

Did you know that you have some level of control over which advertisements are displayed on your blog through Google AdSense? It's far from a perfect system, but the Competitive Ad Filter is certainly better than nothing. The purpose of the Competitive Ad Filter is to block specific ads from appearing on your pages. As its name implies, the Competitive

Ad Filter was originally implemented as a way to block out ads from your direct competitors. For example, if you happen to run an online store that sells running shoes by Nike, you will probably want to block out the advertisements from stores that sell Reebok, Adidas, and Puma shoes. Alternatively, if your run an automotive blog and you've managed to score some private advertising from Quaker State, they may request that ads from other major oil companies not appear on the same page. To use the Competitive Ad Filter, go to your Google AdSense account and prevent the displaying of ads from companies like Pennzoil, Amsoil, and Valvoline. There are many applications for this kind of filter.

Most bloggers don't bother with this option because they assume that opening up the system to all advertisers would provide the best opportunity to make the most money online. Based on the bid system described earlier in this chapter, it may appear that only the highest bids would be able to make it onto your website. Unfortunately, this simply is not the case. Most webmasters assume incorrectly that because they're not AdWords advertisers, they have no competition. If you don't make use of the Competitive Ad Filter, however, you are effectively opening the door for Made For Adsense (MFA) sites and arbitrageurs.

Block Out the Cheap Advertisers

MFA sites have nearly no content whatsoever. Their sole purpose for existing is to make money from Google AdSense. Because they have no real content, MFA sites have very little chance of getting any organic traffic or any traffic from search engines. They have to buy their visitors through Google AdSense and other PPC advertising networks. Naturally, they want to minimize those costs as much as possible, and that's why they will place ad bids for only a couple of pennies per click. If you've ever logged into your AdSense account and saw clicks for a penny or two, there is good chance that it was for an MFA site.

The ad for the MFA site appears on your site and a visitor clicks on it. You make a penny. When the visitor arrives on the MFA site, they are bombarded with a series of much higher-paying advertisements, either from Google AdSense or for some other advertising network. Seeing how this visitor already clicked on one of your ads, they are much more likely than the average visitor to click on yet another ad. When they click on an ad on the MFA site, the MFA site owner makes a dollar or more. If we assume the click values of one cent and one dollar, the MFA site only needs to realize a click-thru rate (CTR) of one percent to break even. With proper implementation and tweaking, these MFA sites can enjoy a CTR much higher than that.

Also known as PPC arbitrage, the process described above can have a serious effect on your AdSense income. Instead of getting more valuable clicks, your blog can become filled with a whole bunch of ads that will only pay a penny or two at a time. You can also imagine that the user experience will be affected, because a site visitor clicks on an ad expecting to get related and relevant content, only to get hit by another page filled with ads. Although you really had little to do with it, this bad experience could reflect poorly on your blog. Google gets paid every time someone clicks on any ad, so they really have no incentive to prevent PPC arbitrage. As long as Google is involved, arbitrageurs are going to stick around.

You want to block out these cheap advertisers so that you can take advantage of the more lucrative ad clicks. You do this with the Competitive Ad Filter.

Adding Sites to the Ad Filter
The assumption is that when you block out the cheap MFA sites, Google will start serving higher paying ads to your site. This won't always be the case, and some of the arbitrageurs will still make it through to your site, but at least you can help to minimize the damage by using the Competitive Ad Filter.

To access the Competitive Ad Filter:
1. Log into your Google AdSense Account.
2. Click on the AdSense Setup tab near the top of the screen.

3. Click on Competitive Ad Filter from the options that show up below the AdSense Setup tab. It's the fifth link from the left.

The URLs that you enter into the Competitive Ad Filter can be as general or as specific as you'd like. For instance, you can block out a domain altogether, preventing all ads leading to example.com from being displayed. You can also block specific sub-domains like blog. example.com, as well as specific pages like blog.example.com/post.html. For the purposes of blocking ads for MFA sites and arbitrageurs, you can probably stick to just the top-level domains. This means that you would block out all ads leading to certain domains. When you enter a URL into the Competitive Ad Filter, this applies to both the display URL (some ads will show the URL below the ad itself), as well as the destination URL (which is where the site visitor actually ends up).

To determine the destination URL of an ad on your blog, you can use the AdSense Preview Tool within the AdSense interface. Do not click on your own ads, because this is a violation of the AdSense Terms of Service (TOS) and *you will be banned from AdSense*. There have been countless publishers who have been banned from AdSense for exactly this reason. They may say that they're innocent, but it doesn't matter. If Google AdSense bans you, you essentially have next to no chance of ever getting accepted again. This isn't the end of the world—there are alternatives—but it can be frustrating, for sure.

A better way to find what MFA sites are advertising on your blog is to make use of a tool called the Ads Black List: http://www.adsblacklist. com. When you enter your blog's URL into their system, Ads Black List will generate a list of fifty MFA sites for you to add to the Competitive Ad Filter. If you become a member of Ads Black List, the generation tool will come up with two hundred MFA sites for you to block. That is the current limit to the Google Competitive Ad Filter, and it's not really enough to block all the MFA sites on the Web. It helps, but it would be nice if Google would expand this limit to a more reasonable number. In addition to the sites provided to you by the Ads Black List,

I also recommend that you add URL-shortening services like tinyurl. com and is.gd to the ad filter. This is because many MFA sites like to hide their URLs by using services like this.

Color Blending

It's a common misconception that you can just take the default Google AdSense layout and throw it onto just about any website. This is far from being the most effective way to implement your ads! It is of critical importance that you play with not only the placement and sizing of the ads, but also with the color scheme. There are two conflicting schools of thought on the matter of adjusting the colors of Google AdSense ads (or just ads in general), and both are equally valid. You will have to do a little experimenting on your blog, because different niches and different site designs perform differently.

The first school of thought says that the ads should be blended in with the existing color scheme of your website. This means that if the text link color for your main content is blue, then the clickable area of the AdSense ad should also be blue. If your blog is predominately red and orange, then your ads should have a similar color scheme. This is because you want the ads to blend in well with the overall look of your site, just as you want the header image and other elements to blend in well with one another. Many webmasters have enjoyed a fair level of success by making the AdSense ads look like navigational links on their sites. This is particularly effective with the AdSense link units, which are really only a series of keywords that will then lead the visitor to a page filled with related ads.

The other school of thought says that the ads should jump out at the site visitor because you want them to pay attention to the ads. After all, if a visitor to your blog doesn't notice the ads on your site, it's unlikely that he or she will click on them either. Remember, you only get paid when someone clicks on an ad. This is in sharp contrast to the CPM (cost per thousand impressions) ad system that is based on page views. By having the AdSense ads featured so prominently, site visitors are more likely to pay attention to them and, thus, they say that the visitors are more likely to click on them.

I personally subscribe more to the first school of thought, not only from a user experience point of view, but also because I seem to enjoy a better click-thru rate when the ads are blended in properly. The ads might not jump out at the site visitor, but you may not necessarily want that to happen anyway. Think about the last time you visited a website that just bombarded you with advertising. Surely, this wasn't a pleasant experience and it's unlikely that you returned to that site. The same can be said about your blog if the advertising is too prominent. Site visitors might not click through, because they might not stick around. Alternatively, some people make a distinct effort to not click on ads, so if they notice the ads, they'll make an effort to avoid them. Contrast this to well-blended ads. The same people who try to avoid clicking on ads may click on one of the units because they feel that it could provide relevant information.

Perhaps the best strategy of all is to find some sort of middle ground between the two. You want the color scheme of the Google AdSense ad units to be in line with the overall color scheme of your blog, but you also want them to be eye-catching enough that a site visitor has a greater chance of noticing (and clicking) on the ads. In my experience, ensuring that the clickable text in the ad unit is the same color as the text links in your blog is of the greatest importance. Generally speaking, the removal of the border is also a good idea. For instance, if the background where you place the ad is white, then you should make the border white too.

Keep an Eye on the Terms of Service

In your effort to optimize the performance of Google AdSense on your blog, I encourage you to be creative. Don't be afraid to experiment with different layout possibilities and color schemes because you may be surprised by which ad styles perform the best. For my blog, the color-blended inline 300×250 pixel box worked the best, but this may not be the case for every blog. As with all things like this, you should follow what the data tells you. Set up different channels for the different ad styles and placements, tracking which perform the best and which perform the worst.

Being creative is one thing. Violating the Google AdSense Terms of Service (TOS) is another matter altogether. It may seem attractive in the short run to bend their rules because it may seem like you'll get a better click-thru rate and make more money as a result. In the long run, this will ultimately work against you. If Google catches you breaking their Terms of Service—like clicking on your own ads—they will ban you from the service. Very rarely do they provide any sort of explanation and even rarer is the opportunity to get back into the system. If you're banned, you're pretty much banned for life.

Besides clicking on your own ads, one of the most common violations is placing images directly next to the ads. Google says that this tricks site visitors into thinking that the pictures are directly related to the content of the ad units. They see the picture of a Nintendo Wii and then there's an ad for a store selling the Nintendo Wii, for instance. They say that this is unfair to the advertiser. Whether you agree with this line of thought or not is of minimal importance to Google. All they care about is that you follow their rules. One of the more recent changes to AdSense involves the inclusion of a Privacy Policy on every publisher's website. Some webmasters may not have noticed this change to the TOS. Be sure to read the Terms of Service carefully!

Chapter Eleven:
My Top Moneymakers

It's easy enough to point at Google AdSense as a recommended ad network for most blogs, especially when you're first starting out and you don't have the traffic numbers for some of the larger, more lucrative ad options. A common mistake that many beginners make is to rely solely on Google AdSense for their blog monetization strategy. If I were to stick only to AdSense, John Chow Dot Com would not be making nearly as much money as it does today. It'd barely be able to make 10% of its current revenue. You're leaving a lot of money on the table by relying solely on AdSense. Don't be a one trick pony.

Through my journeys making money online, I have come across countless other advertising platforms and not all of them have been lucrative. Based on my experience, I have compiled a list of a few advertising networks that are proven moneymakers. They are not only lucrative, but they are also reliable. You don't want to invest in a fly-by-night operation.

TTZ Media
http://www.ttzmedia.com

As you might be able to guess from its name, TTZ Media is my own ad network and it was originally formed for the TechZone (refer to chapter 2 for more about that site). The ad platform has grown and matured considerably over the years; originally, it was exclusive to the sites of people who I knew personally, and then, within the last year or so I opened up TTZ Media to the general public. TTZ Media is an ad network that is best suited for technology and shopping-related websites because it displays ads for mostly technology-related products. The products displayed in the ads include digital cameras, portable GPS navigation devices, laptop computers, video games, and other related items.

The products come up in the TTZ Media ads are based on the keywords provided by the publisher. For example, if your blog is all about cell phones, you can enter "cell phone" into the keyword area of the TTZ Media administration panel, and the code generated will produce ads that featured cell phone-related products. There are price comparisons, ratings, and other ad creatives that provide value to the site visitor. They may not necessarily see it as an ad, because it looks like the website is providing them with a useful service, shopping around on their behalf. When readers click on an item, they are then directed to the online store where the product is sold at the price displayed in the ad.

The revenue model is CPC, or cost-per-click. This means that every time a reader clicks on one of the ads, you get paid a set amount of money. The CPC rates are determined by product categories and the number of clicks that you are able to generate. The more traffic you are able to send to the affiliate stores, the higher your click value will be. This provides extra incentive for increasing your traffic and improving your click-thru rate.

Unlike Google AdSense, there is no bid system in place with TTZ Media, so every click is worth exactly the same amount of money. Also, unlike affiliate programs and other CPA-based (cost-per-action) ad networks, site visitors do not actually need to complete a purchase for you to get paid. All the reader has to do is click on the ad. Performance will vary, of course, but many tech review sites often realize eCPM (effective cost-per-thousand) as high as $12. This means that for every 1000 page views, these sites are generating $12 in revenue. Multiply that through by the number of page views in a month (higher traffic sites can get millions of views a month) and you've got yourself a healthy level of income.

ReviewMe

http://www.reviewme.com/

ReviewMe serves as a very considerable contributor to the monthly income of John Chow Dot Com. With ReviewMe, advertisers purchase sponsored reviews on your blog. They can provide you with a physical product, but more often than not, the subject of the review will be something that is online. This could be another blog (you can order reviews through ReviewMe too), an online store, or some sort of online service. In the past, I have reviewed paid wiki sites, online file storage solutions, and the blogs of several individuals.

Just because they are paying you to review their product or service does not mean that the review has to be positive. As part of the ReviewMe guidelines, all reviews should be as objective as possible. You can be as negative or as positive as you'd like in your review, as long as it's two hundred words. It is also important that you have some level of disclosure in the post, telling readers that it is a paid review, but that your opinions are still honest and not swayed by the fact that you are getting paid to write the review.

The ReviewMe marketplace sets the price of a review on your blog based on your blog's rankings in Alexa and Technorati, as well as your estimated number of RSS subscribers. Bigger blogs with better traffic numbers attract a higher price point because an advertiser gets a much higher level of exposure. If you don't like the price set by ReviewMe, you can manually edit your paid review price to whatever you'd like. Bear in mind that ReviewMe takes a 50% revenue share, so if you set a price of $100 for a review on your blog, for example, the payout is $50.

Text Link Ads

http://www.text-link-ads.com/

It's important to diversify the monetization methods on your blog. When most people think of advertising, they picture the various sizes of banners that populate a website. With Text Link Ads, the advertising is a little subtler. In the sidebar of John Chow Dot Com, you may notice that there is a section called Featured Sites. All the sites mentioned in this section are actual paid advertisements. The advertisers pay a monthly fee in order to have a link to their website featured on my blog. This offers the advertisers a good level of exposure as well as some search engine benefits. Readers of your blog won't mind these additional links, because they are not at all intrusive; they're just text links.

In addition to these sidebar links that appear site wide, Text Link Ads is also able to sell post-level ads. They insert a single sentence at the end of a chosen article on your blog that contains a link back to the advertiser. This sentence is usually labeled as a "Related Link" or something similar. From a reader's point of view, this may not necessarily be seen as advertising either because the link could provide useful supplementary information. Advertisers can target blog posts that are particularly relevant to their products and services.

PepperJam Network

http://www.pepperjamnetwork.com

As you grow the user base of your blog, largely represented by the number of subscribers to your RSS feed, you can make some serious money through affiliate marketing. This is a monetization strategy that can be more difficult for smaller blogs because it's a numbers game. With affiliate marketing, you only get paid when a site visitor completes a certain action. This could be subscribing to the advertiser's newsletter, making a purchase on the advertiser's website, or doing any number of other things that the advertiser may specify. For example, a company like Netflix may offer a payout when you refer someone to them who signs up for a free trial. Simply clicking on the ad is not enough.

One of the major issues with affiliate marketing is that it can be very troublesome to sign up for each of the individual referral programs from all those different companies. Netflix has a referral/affiliate program, Blockbuster has one, BlueFur web hosting has one, as do many others; you would need to sign up for each program individually, which takes a lot of time. And that's where PepperJam steps in. Instead of signing up for hundreds of affiliate accounts, you just sign up for a single account with PepperJam Network, and you have access to all of them.

Founded by my friend Kris Jones, PepperJam Network amalgamates all of these affiliate programs into a single marketplace. You can browse through the different deals and advertise whichever referral program you'd like. This is a great way to get started with affiliate marketing because you can experiment with different companies and ad creatives. The creation of PepperJam Network took eight years of research and development. Kris Jones didn't do it alone; he pulled together the ideas, feedback, and intelligence of *hundreds* of professional affiliate marketers and advertisers. Implemented correctly, affiliate marketing can easily be one of your blog's biggest moneymakers.

Kontera ContentLink

http://www.kontera.com/

As you may have noticed, the pages on your blog only have so much available real estate. If you were to populate every page with a countless number of ad banners, you would effectively leave yourself no room for actual content. The user experience would probably suffer considerably as well. This is one of the biggest reasons why you shouldn't put all your eggs in one basket, and why you should look into different ways to monetize your blog in addition to the standard ad banners and buttons. The great thing about Kontera ContentLink is that it doesn't take up any additional room on your blog, yet it can be a substantial moneymaker.

With Kontera, can insert advertising into your blog posts, but these ads do not need any space of their own. The Kontera ContentLink technology reads your posts and automatically transforms certain words in the post into ads. This is similar, in some ways, to when you provide a link within your blog post to either another one of your posts or to an external source. The Kontera links are distinguishable from regular links because they are double-underlined. When a user hovers his or her mouse pointer over one of these double-underlined words, an ad floats above your content. If clicked, the visitor is then directed to the advertiser's website, and you make money for referring that visitor.

Normally, Kontera has rather stringent requirements for the publishers that they include in their program. For instance, the site must have a minimum of five hundred thousand page views per month. Needless to say, most beginning bloggers will not be able to achieve this level of traffic from the get-go. Because I have a special relationship with Kontera, we have worked out an agreement allows smaller blogs to use the ContentLink service. When you are filling out the application form, enter "John Chow Kontera partnership" into the Comments field, and the application will be sent to my personal account representative. He will review (and hopefully approve) your application based on the quality of your blog content rather than your traffic level.

Bidvertiser
http://www.bidvertiser.com/

Bidvertiser is a great alternative to Google AdSense, especially for smaller publishers who are having a hard time reaching the $100 minimum payout level of AdSense. Bidvertiser, like AdSense, is a contextual cost-per-click (CPC) ad network. This means that you get paid each time a site visitor clicks on one of the ads. Also like AdSense, advertisers on Bidvertiser bid against one another for certain keywords. In this way, bloggers and website owners have a better chance at getting advertisements that are the high-paying; competition among the advertisers tends to push the per-click costs higher.

Among the key advantages that Bidvertiser has over other CPC ad networks like Google AdSense, the minimum payout level is just

$10. You may have a difficult time reaching the magic $100 level with AdSense, but getting to ten dollars on Bidvertiser could be easier. Furthermore, you can accept payment from Bidvertiser through PayPal, which is extremely convenient.

Another advantage of Bidvertiser is its high level of ad customization. Other networks may allow you to adjust the color scheme, but it usually doesn't go much further than that. With Bidvertiser, not only can you change the colors, you can also adjust the font, the text size, and the actual dimensions of the ad creatives. This effectively lets bloggers and publishers fully customize their ads for optimal integration; the theoretically infinite number of ad sizes is certainly appealing.

Azoogle Ads

http://www.azoogleads.com/

Vonage. VistaPrint. Blockbuster Total Access. What do these companies have in common? They all offer their affiliate program through Azoogle Ads, one of the largest performance-based online advertising networks in the world. The key advantages to Azoogle Ads are very similar to those of the PepperJam Network described above, meaning that you'll have access to a huge library of affiliate offers that you can advertise through your blog. They offer some of the best and highest-paying affiliate deals in the industry, and the variety is absolutely astounding. It doesn't really matter what topic your blog covers because you'll surely find a deal that matches your site.

Payout levels vary depending on the advertiser and the extent of the action required from the site visitor, but you can receive payouts of over $100 per action. That's a lot of money, which explains why affiliate marketing is on the biggest moneymakers for John Chow Dot Com. Azoogle Ads is perfectly compatible with PepperJam Ads, so it's a great idea to sign up with both ad networks so that you can have access to a simply monstrous number of affiliate deals. In my experience, Azoogle Ads offers some of the best payouts in the business; you just have to market the deals effectively.

ShoppingAds

http://shoppingads.com/

ShoppingAds started life as AuctionAds. At the time, AuctionAds was a really big eBay affiliate. Few people seem to know that eBay has an affiliate program, which is based on referring people to auctions and requiring them to win the auctions. The person who refers the successful bidder makes a portion of the fees that eBay collects from the sale. The size of this portion depends on the volume of successful bids that the affiliate refers to eBay. As you can imagine, it can be difficult to move up to the higher volume levels on your own. This was where AuctionAds was supposed to step into the picture, because it put all of the AuctionAds publishers into one big "collective," effectively moving everyone into the higher revenue share bracket.

Bloggers could still advertise through the eBay affiliate program, but they would be doing it through AuctionAds, potentially earning a much larger revenue share than they would be able to achieve on their own. Furthermore, AuctionAds came with its own ad delivery system, which included ad creatives that could highlight specific auctions, showing the current bid price and an image of the item. These auctions could be selected based on keywords; there was also a tool that would allow you to select a specific auction.

When AuctionAds was transformed into ShoppingAds, it maintained similar ad creatives and a similar ad delivery system. The difference was that they added a CPC ad system that was overlaid on top of the CPA (cost-per-action) system of the eBay affiliate program. In this way, the ads served could generate income on a per-click basis or on a per-action basis. The CPA ads were still through the eBay affiliate program, but the CPC ads would send visitors directly to an advertiser's online store. It's almost like the best of both worlds.

Chapter Twelve:
Private Ad Sales

In this chapter, I will discuss the single largest source of income on John Chow Dot Com: direct ad sales.

The biggest disadvantage to using ad networks is that they inevitably take a cut out of your revenue. If they take a 50% revenue share, for example, it means that your blog is actually earning twice as much as you think you are. Popular ad networks like Google AdSense and Text Link Ads, for example, are known for taking a 50% revenue share. This means that when an advertiser pays $100 for a text link on your blog, you only see $50. This commission paid to the advertising network is a necessary evil when you're first starting out with your blog because you won't be able to attract advertisers to a new blog right away. The ad networks deliver the advertisers for you through their online marketplaces.

As your blog becomes bigger and more well-known, however, you may want to slowly move away from ad networks towards direct sales. Private ad sales are easily the single biggest source of income for John Chow Dot Com, responsible for over half of all the money taken in by my blog. There are advantages and disadvantages to direct ad sales, but in the end, the upside generally outweighs the downside. The main upside is that you will be able to make more money, assuming that you are able to maintain the same level of advertising on your blog. The downside is that you may have to deal with customer service and ad-serving issues that would otherwise be taken care of by the ad network.

Even so, I recommend that you move toward private ad sales when your blog is ready. But how can you tell when your blog is ready?

Traffic Comes First, Private Ads Come Later

If your blog is only attracting a modest level of traffic, there is no reason why an advertiser would want to purchase advertising directly from you. Furthermore, it's unlikely that you will be attracting enough attention to even have potential advertisers notice you in the first place. Think about it from an advertiser's point of view: they'll more likely want to advertise on a big blog (if they can afford it) than a blog that only has a handful of visitors each day. Without enough traffic, there really is no point in taking the direct ad sales route since you won't be able to charge much for the ads anyway. You're better off sticking with AdSense and other ad networks until you have enough traffic.

When your blog is still relatively new, it's a much better strategy to focus your energy on creating quality content and developing traffic. Spending all that time trying to develop sales is not going to be very fruitful because ad sales won't happen without traffic. In your effort to develop a higher level of traffic, it might even be a good idea to forgo advertising altogether until you are able to attract a consistently high number of visitors on a daily basis. John Chow Dot Com did not have any advertising on it for its first nine months!

Work on developing traffic first. Without traffic, your blog might as well not exist.

Create an Advertising Page

When you are ready to take the plunge into the lucrative world of direct ad sales, one of the most critical things you'll need to do is to make an advertising page. Without a page on your blog that explicitly states that you're selling private advertising, there's no way for any potential advertisers to know that they can buy ad space from you. Also, many bloggers seem to think that an "advertise here" page is meant to generate leads that you can follow up on. I beg to differ. I believe that your advertising page should be enough to get the sale.

This is largely a matter of time management. Dealing with all the inquiries and negotiating different advertising deals can be a seriously time-consuming activity. It's unlikely that you're going to hire a sales and marketing team to handle this aspect of your blog for you, so you want the process to be as automated as possible. This way, you can spend your time on creating quality content rather than negotiating and dealing with advertisers. If all the pertinent information is completely spelled out on your "advertise here" page, you weed out most of the advertisers who just wanted to get a price or those who wanted to know what ad options were available.

Your advertising page should consist of the following elements:

1. Traffic stats and other metrics: Advertisers want to know how much exposure they're going to get from advertising on your blog. There is a huge difference between buying an ad banner on a blog that gets one hundred thousand unique visitors each day and one that only gets one hundred visitors a day. This will help advertisers determine whether the prices on your blog are "worth it." These traffic stats and other information should be placed right at the top of your advertising page. This is akin to the advertising page for a magazine, which describes the size of the reader base and distribution up front. Your blog should be much the same. Among the data that you should include in this section are page views and unique visitors (monthly stats are usually best), target audience, Alexa rank, Technorati rank, number of RSS subscribers, and anything else that you think a potential advertiser should know. It's also important to establish trust, so you may want to show screenshots from

Google Analytics (or some other stat-tracking service), as well as links to your Alexa and Technorati pages.

2. Description of all your advertising options: When most visitors come to your blog, they will assume that only banner and button advertising will be accepted. These are easily the most visible and explicit forms of advertising. The job of your advertising page is to explain all of the advertising options, including the banner you may have in the header, the ad boxes you may embed into each post, the text links you sell in the sidebar, and the footer ads you may include in the RSS feed. Be creative and come up with some new options for advertisers. Mention the possibility of having a paid review. Describe the specifics of each ad placement and don't forget to include your ad prices as well. This helps to eliminate a lot of time because you won't have to spend all of your time responding to e-mails that are simply looking for pricing. This also helps to eliminate the need for communicating with people who think that your advertising prices are too high. If they want to lowball you on your rates, they probably aren't worth your time.

3. Testimonials from past advertisers: Don't go too far with this, but including a few testimonials from past advertisers can go a long way toward landing a sale. Getting past advertisers to put in a kind word about how well their ads performed on your blog can convince potential advertisers to take the plunge. Remember that advertisers tend to follow the crowd; if they see that other people have been happy with advertising on your blog, and if they're convinced of the results others have received, they're more likely to purchase advertising from you. It may be helpful to do a case study with one advertiser in particular, writing a blog post about his conversion rate, increase in traffic, and so on. Ask for permission first, of course. After completing this blog post, you can link on the post to your advertising page.

If your blog has been named on any prominent list (best new blogger, best blog about whatever, etc.), it is also a good idea to include this information on your advertise page, because it gives you a certain level of prestige and credibility. When describing the different advertising options, try to be as specific as possible: tell advertisers exactly where the ad will be placed, and be up front about your restrictions. For example, you may allow banners comprised of animated GIF images, but you may not allow Flash. It's also a good idea to limit the file size on ad banners so that you can have greater control over your bandwidth.

How to Set the Prices

In the process of setting up your advertising page, you might start to wonder what sort of prices you should be charging for advertising on your blog. After all, if this is your first attempt at private advertising; you don't want to price yourself out of the market, but you also don't want to sell yourself short. Well, before you do anything else, it's probably in your best interest to get rid of Google AdSense, or at least remove it from the pages on which you'd like to sell advertising. AdSense has a system called Google SiteMatch. These SiteMatch ads are a form of Google AdSense ads that appear on only one specific site. The advertiser selects one site in particular and their ads will appear on that site and no others. It's a form of direct advertising, except it is through the Google AdSense/AdWords system, meaning that Google gets its cut.

If we assume a 50% revenue share—Google has never stated explicitly how much of a cut they take out of ads sold through the Google AdSense system—advertisers can find a "back door" to cheap advertising on a highly-prized blog. For a while, I was able to purchase advertising on Problogger.net using Google SiteMatch. My average cost was about $2.50 CPM, which is exceptionally cheap for a 300×250 p ad block on a site as popular as Problogger. Darren Rowse, the site's owner, could have easily sold advertising in that exact same spot for much more than $2.50 CPM. The thing is that Darren doesn't get the full $2.50. If we assume that 50% revenue share, this means that Darren would only receive $1.25 CPM. By going with private advertising, he would eliminate this cut and he could increase his CPM to a more reasonable level.

When you get ready to sell direct ads on your blog, you will probably want to bid adieu to Google AdSense. Close that back door and reap the full rewards.

The easiest way to decide how much you should charge for advertising on your blog is to take a look at the average eCPM that the ad placement is currently generating with Google AdSense. When you log into your AdSense account, you can look back on quite a lengthy period of time for stats. This is why you should have set up different channels for your ads so that you can track their individual performances. To calculate how much to charge for a 468×60 pixel banner that you have near the header image, for example, you would go through the following steps.

1. Log into your Google AdSense account and look at the eCPM for that placement in the last few months.
2. Take a look at your site statistics to see how many page views your blog had over the same period of time.
3. Multiply the eCPM by the average number of monthly page views on your blog.
4. Divide this number by one thousand, because eCPM is based on one thousand page views.
5. The resulting figure is how much your blog made from that ad placement in one month.
6. Take this number and *at least* double it.

If you are earning $2.00 per thousand ad impressions, it means that Google is charging $4.00 (assuming a 50% revenue share). By extension, if that ad placement has earned you $50 a month on average, it means that Google is charging $100 for that ad placement. There's no reason why you would sell the ad spot privately for any less than double because that's what Google is selling it for. If you're really ambitious, you can try charging a fair bit more than double because the AdSense ads could be undervaluing the traffic on your blog. Another way to make even more money is to implement an ad rotation system (more on this later in the chapter), selling the ad placement to several advertisers simultaneously. This is the strategy that I have employed with the majority of ad placements on John Chow Dot Com.

Another thing to keep in mind is that it's sometimes better to use an ad placement for an affiliate deal than for a direct ad sale. It's possible that you could earn a lot more money from the ad through affiliate commissions than you would through a straight sale. For example, I could sell an ad button to Text Link Ads for $500 a month, but I would be giving up over $2,000 in Text Link Ads affiliate income. I make more money promoting their network through affiliate commissions than I would through a direct sale.

Sold Out on the First Day

One thing that you have to remember is that advertisers are still people and they will inevitably have the tendency to follow the crowd. If you choose to offer six 125x125 pixel squares in your blog's sidebar, for example, the worst thing you can do is to occupy all six ad locations with a placeholder that says that advertising is available on your site. This shows that you currently have no support from any advertisers, and most advertisers will think that it's not a good idea to buy advertising on your blog. After all, why should they buy advertising from you if no one else is doing it? This is a common mistake that many beginning bloggers make when they first start to sell private advertising.

What should you do to occupy those spaces until advertisers do come on board? Simply make it look like the ad placements are being sold by placing affiliate links and other forms of advertising in those squares. When you sign up for an affiliate network like Azoogle Ads or Pepperjam Network, you will likely find some affiliate deals in there that have predesigned 125x125 pixel buttons. Use these to fill the space until you are able to attract enough direct ad sales. Never utilize more than one of these ad placements to tell site visitors that they can advertise on your site. If you use any more than one, you are not only giving up potential revenue through affiliate sales and other advertising, but you are also showing the world that it's not really worthwhile to advertise on your blog. I'm using the popular 125x125 p button as an example, but the same can be said about a 468x60 pixel banner, a 160x600 pixel skyscraper ad, or any other ad creative. Text link ads are no exception. If you don't have any sales happening either directly or through Text Link Ads, fill those text link spaces with affiliate links.

Naturally, the ideal situation is to sell all your ad locations on the first day that you offer private advertising. This was exactly the case with John Chow Dot Com when I decided to roll out a new blog theme. Before the new ad spots were opened up—most notably the eight 125x125 p ad buttons—I sent out an e-mail to some of the previous advertisers who had purchased ReviewMe reviews on John Chow Dot Com. By approaching people who had previously purchased advertising on my blog, I knew that I was getting a more targeted audience and the chances that they would be interested in buying advertising directly from me would be substantially higher. This is a much more effective method for conversion that cold calling (or cold e-mailing, as the case may be), because previous advertisers have already experienced the benefits of advertising on my blog.

The original blog redesign only called for six ad locations in the sidebar, all buttons of the 125x125 pixel variety. I sent out an e-mail to ten past advertisers, providing them with a screenshot of the new theme and the new ad placement. In the e-mail, I asked if they wanted to be the first to sponsor my blog on the new theme. Of the ten advertisers that I approached, I hoped that six would buy ads. As luck would have it, I ended up with eight sales. The theme was slightly expanded and I effectively did even better than selling out on the first day!

The take-home lesson here is that it's *a lot* easier to sell to someone who has dealt with you before than it is to make a brand-new sale. This is why so many companies work so hard to maintain existing customers; it's a lot cheaper to keep a customer than it is to find a new one. When the time comes for you to start selling direct ads, start with the sites and advertisers that you are currently dealing with (or have already dealt with) and work from there. If you notice that there are some SiteMatch advertisers in your Google AdSense, it might be worthwhile to approach them as well. Like the advertisers who you already know, these SiteMatch advertisers recognize the value of buying advertising from your blog. Tell them that you are removing AdSense ads, and if they want to continue advertising on your blog, they'll have to deal directly with you. It's a win-win situation for everyone involved.

The Best Ad Management System: OIOpublisher Direct

http://www.oiopublisher.com

I've always recommended that new bloggers should use ad networks when they are first starting out with a monetized blog. Until you reach a certain level of traffic, it's not only very difficult to attract the attention of advertisers, but the rates that you would be able to charge for private advertising are relatively low. It wouldn't be worth the hassle. There's a significant amount of extra work involved with selling private ads, not to mention the countless customer service headaches that could be involved. You have to deal with the advertisers, handle payments, upload the ad creatives, and make sure you take down their advertising when their payment period ends. For all this work, it might not sound like it's worth going through the trouble of direct ad sales at all.

Thankfully, there is a fantastic piece of software that automates the entire ad-buying process on your blog. You don't have to deal with handling payments. You don't have to keep track of when advertisement periods commence and end. You don't have to worry about managing the different ad banners and text links because all of that stuff is completely automatic with this piece of software. In doing this, you are granted more time to concentrate on blogging and creating quality content, rather than handling the sales and customer service aspects of selling private advertising.

This piece of software is OIOpublisher Direct. This WordPress script is the best way for a blogger to sell his ad space privately because it really does take care of the entire ad sale process. When installed and implemented, OIOpublisher Direct can act as a virtual sales associate for your blog. Advertisers click on the appropriate link and then they can order, pay for, and upload their ads directly to your blog. The forms are very easy to use and the only thing that you have to do is approve the ad. The best part is that this WordPress script can be installed on an unlimited number of domains and it is able to automatically process the payments through a PayPal subscription.

You can find out more information about the WordPress script through this splash page too: http://splash.oiopublisher.com. There's also a live demo of how OIOpublisher Direct works, both from a publisher's and from an advertiser's point of view. These give you a hands-on experience with what it would be like for an advertiser to purchase advertising on your blog through the OIOpublisher Direct, as well as how it would look like from the blog owner's point of view. The demo can be found here: http://demo.oiopublisher.com

Considering everything that OIOpublisher Direct is able to do and the amount of time that it will save you, you'd imagine that this piece of software would be quite pricey. It's a very powerful WordPress script, so it is a little surprising that they sell it for just $37. You should be able to make your money back within the first ad sale or two because you get to keep 100% of your sales revenue with private ad sales sold through the OIOpublisher Direct system; they do not take any further commission beyond the original $37 purchase price. There is not a doubt in my mind that this is the most comprehensive WordPress ad management tool around. If you can't make the $37 back, you really don't belong in this business.

Chapter Thirteen:
The Formula for Success

In this chapter, we tie everything together and provide a complete picture for making money from blogging.

Congratulations on taking the first and most important step toward success as a professional blogger. Now that you've read through many of the key techniques and strategies that I employ to make over $30,000 a month from my personal blog, it's time for you to go out there and do it yourself. There really is no time like the present. Don't wait for the conditions and circumstances to be perfect because they never will be. There will always be *something* that you think is holding you back. Don't let this get in your way.

Each blog is a little different, and what might work for one site might not be quite as effective for another site. That said, there are at least five elements that are common to most successful blogs. This is by no means a summary of everything that you need to know about successful blogging, but these elements will certainly point you in the right direction.

1. Quality Content
It always starts with quality content. Without quality content, your blog really doesn't exist. Whether you decide to blog about fast cars

or basketball, computers or celebrities, the most important thing that you need to keep in mind is that all of your articles should be of high quality and offer something useful and original to your readers. You are not CNN, nor should you try to be.

People come to a blog for its human aspect, and they come to your blog for *your* opinion because the most unique thing about your blog is you. Don't just regurgitate the same information and the same ideas that you find on every other blog in your niche because you will never be able to stand out from the crowd that way. You need to be unique.

Your articles might provide something actually useful to your readers. They might provide a great dose of comedy. Whatever the case may be, you want your content to be good enough that people will want to come back on a regular basis for more. If your content sucks, they won't come back.

2. Marketing Skills

Great content is one thing; there are lots of great writers out there. The trouble is that a lot of great writers have no idea how to market themselves. While your primary focus should be on producing some top-notch articles for your blog, you need to also pay attention to getting other people to notice them. Some of the most successful bloggers on the Web are not necessarily successful because of what they have to say; they're successful because of how they have managed to position themselves on the Internet and how they have managed to market their blog accordingly. The same can be said about just about any product on the marketplace. The Apple iPod's success is largely a result of a fantastic marketing blitz. Steve Jobs and the rest of the team in Cupertino know a lot about marketing.

One of the better strategies that you can employ in marketing your own blog is to get involved in social networking sites and other online communities. Take advantage of social bookmarking services like Digg, StumbleUpon, and Propeller. Participate in forums in your niche so that you can establish yourself as an expert. Comment on other blogs in your niche to further expand your online presence. Also, when you're ready to take the plunge into paid advertising for your blog, make sure that you have a specific objective in mind. Is it to increase RSS subscribers? Increase the number of comments? Improve the conversion rate on a particular affiliate deal?

Perhaps one of the most crucial elements to marketing is branding. Your blog should have its own distinct identity, and it should be one that people will immediately recognize. When technology bloggers hear "root of all evil," they immediately think of me. That's because I've branded myself as the root of all evil. Establish *your* blogging brand and stand out from the millions of other blogs on the Web. What makes you special or different?

3. Dedication

I hear it all the time. People get inspired by what I have managed to do with John Chow Dot Com and they feel inspired to start a blog of their own. They get off to a fantastic start, pumping out all sorts of fantastic content for the first couple of weeks, and they feel really excited about the prospects of making money from their blog. And then the reality of low traffic numbers hits them and they no longer feel quite as motivated to keep up the same level of content production, going from multiple posts per day to barely updating the blog at all. These blogs, as you can imagine, never take off, and their owners feel that blogging for money is a lost cause.

Don't be one of these people.

It's important that you are dedicated to your goals and are willing to suffer through the low times. When your blog is first starting out, you will not have thousands of RSS subscribers. When your blog is first starting out, it's unlikely that it's going to rank for anything in search engines like Google. Don't be discouraged. Perhaps the single greatest attribute of a success entrepreneur—and a professional blogger is an entrepreneur like any other—is dedication. Be dedicated to your goals and be willing to follow through. If I got discouraged by the first month of income from John Chow Dot Com, I would have never been able to make more than a few hundred dollars a month from the blog. I stuck with it and looked for ways to improve. I looked at how I could make the blog better, more prominent, and ultimately more successful. Be dedicated to your craft and success will follow.

4. Adaptability

Just because I say that you should be dedicated does not mean that I am telling you to be stubborn. If a particular strategy for traffic generation isn't working, for example, then it could be time for you to try something new. The Internet is not static; it's an incredibly dynamic beast that changes from year to year, month to month, moment to moment. When I first launched the TechZone years ago, there really wasn't such a thing as a cost-per-click advertising network. Advertising on any given website was based solely on impressions (CPM), so there was no motivation for webmasters to optimize the ads. We didn't care if visitors clicked on the ads or not. This is a sharp contrast to the countless CPC and CPA (cost-per-action)-based ad networks of today. I had to adapt and learn about Google AdSense. I had to learn about how to optimize the ads to maximize the click-thru rate. If I stuck with the old-school mentality, I would not be as successful as I am today. Not even close.

You must be willing to adapt and keep up with the times. Digg might be popular today and it might be a great source of traffic for your blog, but that could change tomorrow. Before Google came around, many people turned to Yahoo! for their Web search needs. I need not remind you that Google absolutely dominates that market today. Each search engine works in a slightly different way and you have to be willing to learn how to work the system in your favor. Those who don't adapt are the first to die off.

5. Maximizing Revenue

The fifth and final element to making money from a blog, ironically enough, is the part about actually making money.

The weight loss industry is a multi-billion dollar business, but with all the money people spend on diet pills and other products, the key to losing weight can be summed up in four simple words: *Eat less, exercise more*. The key to making money from a blog is much the same. It too can be summed in four simple words: *Get traffic, optimize revenue*. Everything that I do on John Chow Dot Com is meant to either get traffic or to optimize revenue.

Why do you want to rank in Google for certain terms? That's to get traffic. Why do you want to increase comments or produce quality content? That's to get traffic too. Why did I get a site redesign about a year into monetizing the blog? Why did I decide to eventually abandon AdSense and take the route of private advertising instead? I did these things to optimize revenue. It's only when you consider both of these concepts that you will be able to have a truly successful blog.

You'll soon notice, however, that getting more traffic is a lot more difficult that optimizing your revenue sources. Think of it this way. If you are getting a thousand visitors a day and you are getting an overall eCPM (effective cost per thousand) of $10, you will earn $10 a day. To get yourself to $20 a day, you can either double your traffic or double your eCPM. Believe me when I say that it's a lot easier to try to get more money out of the existing number of visitors than it is to try to increase the number of visitors. The biggest reason why John Chow Dot Com makes so much money is that I was able to maximize the ad revenue, earning a site-wide eCPM of over $100. Not very many sites can say they've done that.

But you can do it, too. You just have to believe you can.

Appendix: Useful Links

John Chow Dot Com
http://www.johnchow.com/

Michael Kwan
http://michaelkwan.com

Beyond the Rhetoric
http://btr.michaelkwan.com/

WordPress
http://wordpress.org/

Fantastico
http://netenberg.com/fantastico.php

Technorati
http://technorati.com/

About the Authors

John Chow is a dot-com mogul from Richmond, British Columbia, Canada. He started out as a partner in a local Richmond printing company before he figured it was time to move on to greener pastures. In April 1999, he decided to launch the TechZone (http://www.thetechzone.com), a website that has become one of the largest hardware tech sites on the Internet. The site has over ten thousand pages of quality content and gets over two hundred thousand page views per day. The self-proclaimed "root of all evil" shares his many techniques to make money online through John Chow Dot Com (http://www.johnchow.com). John Chow has been featured in such publications as The *Vancouver Sun*, the *Globe and Mail, Entrepreneur Magazine, Ming Pao Magazine*, and *BC Business Magazine*.

Michael Kwan is a freelance writer based out of Vancouver, British Columbia, Canada. He graduated with honors from the University of British Columbia with a degree in Psychology and English Literature. During that time, he worked as a contributing writer and co-editor for *Arts@Work*, the official newsletter of the UBC Arts Co-op Program. Today, Michael's freelance work is mostly found online with a focus on professional blogging and technology reviews. His writing has been featured on such popular websites as Mobile Magazine (http://mobilemag.com) and Hadouken Online (http://www.hadoukenonline.com). Michael also maintains his own blog, Beyond the Rhetoric (http://btr.michaelkwan.com), where he writes about personal development and freelance writing, as well as other topics of the day.

FREE BONUS

As a special thank you for buying this book, we'd like to offer you a free bonus video tutorial. Meet the man behind MAKE MONEY ONLINE and learn how he earns over $40,000 a month from a blog.

John Chow gave a special presentation at the Vancouver Business, Marketing and Entrepreneur meetup, describing the specifics of his blog business model, and now this special video is available online.

To gain access to the video tutorial for FREE, go to:

http://www.johnchow.com/bookbonus

No additional purchase is required. This is a free thank you for purchasing this book.

BUY A SHARE OF THE FUTURE IN YOUR COMMUNITY

These certificates make great holiday, graduation and birthday gifts that can be personalized with the recipient's name. The cost of one S.H.A.R.E. or one square foot is $54.17. The personalized certificate is suitable for framing and will state the number of shares purchased and the amount of each share, as well as the recipient's name. The home that you participate in "building" will last for many years and will continue to grow in value.

Here is a sample SHARE certificate:

HABITAT FOR HUMANITY

THIS CERTIFIES THAT

YOUR NAME HERE

HAS INVESTED IN A HOME FOR A DESERVING FAMILY

1985-2005

TWENTY YEARS OF BUILDING FUTURES IN OUR
COMMUNITY ONE HOME AT A TIME

1200 SQUARE FOOT HOUSE @ $65,000 = $54.17 PER SQUARE FOOT
This certificate represents a tax deductible donation. It has no cash value

YES, I WOULD LIKE TO HELP!

I support the work that Habitat for Humanity does and I want to be part of the excitement! As a donor, I will receive periodic updates on your construction activities but, more importantly, I know my gift will help a family in our community realize the dream of homeownership. **I would like to SHARE in your efforts against substandard housing in my community!** *(Please print below)*

PLEASE SEND ME _____ SHARES at $54.17 EACH = $ $_____

In Honor Of: _____

Occasion: (Circle One)   HOLIDAY   BIRTHDAY   ANNIVERSARY

OTHER: _____

Address of Recipient: _____

Gift From: _____ *Donor Address:* _____

Donor Email: _____

I AM ENCLOSING A CHECK FOR $ $_____ PAYABLE TO HABITAT FOR HUMANITY <u>OR</u> PLEASE CHARGE MY VISA OR MASTERCARD *(CIRCLE ONE)*

Card Number _____ Expiration Date: _____

Name as it appears on Credit Card _____ Charge Amount $ _____

Signature _____

Billing Address _____

Telephone # Day _____ Eve _____

PLEASE NOTE: Your contribution is tax-deductible to the fullest extent allowed by law.
Habitat for Humanity • P.O. Box 1443 • Newport News, VA 23601 • 757-596-5553
www.HelpHabitatforHumanity.org